D1486972

PROVENCE

TEXT
SIMONETTA GREGGIO

PHOTOS
HERVÉ CHAMPOLLION

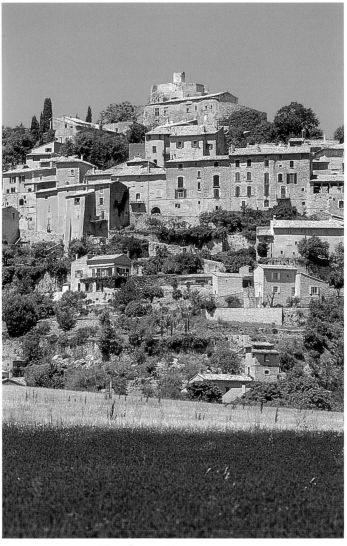

Translation: Entreprises 35

Éditions Ouest-France

s u m m a r y

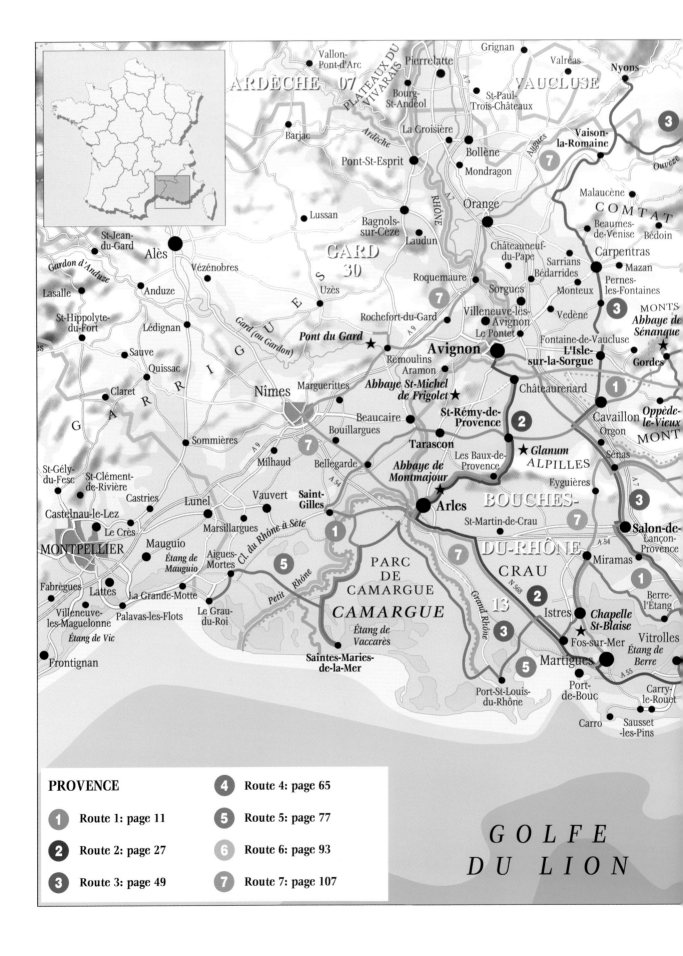

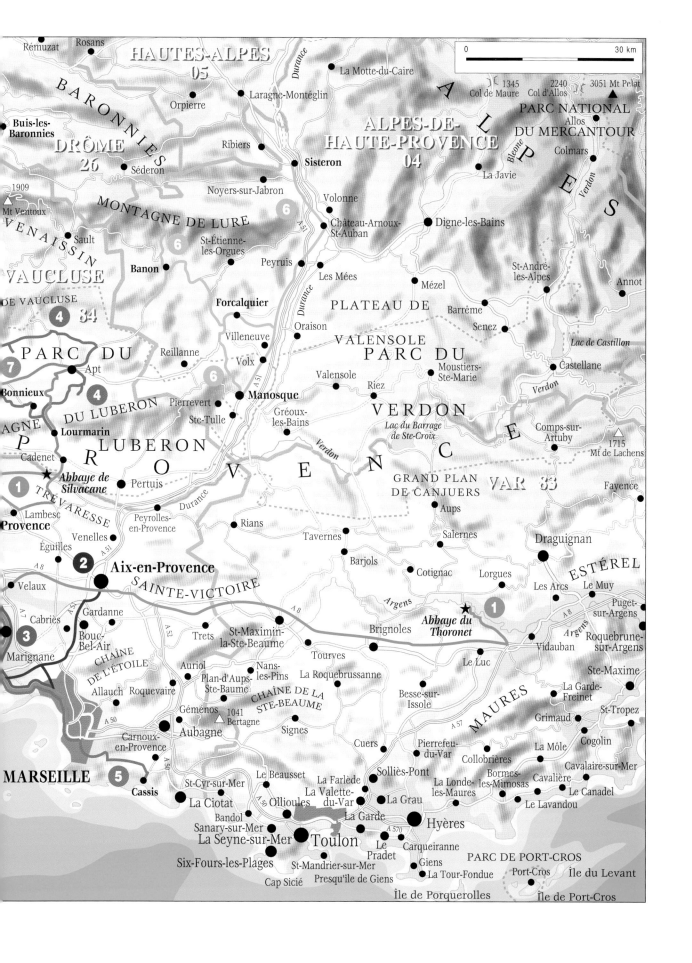

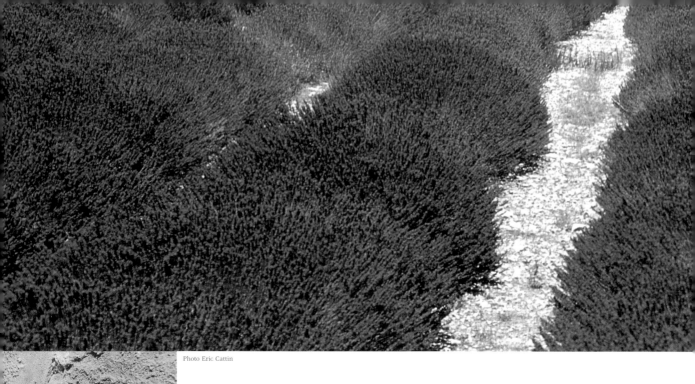

Photo Eric Cattin

𝒯he much vaunted beauty of Provence is part also of its generosity, its quality of life, its savours and its odours.

Whether it comes from a siesta under an olive tree after a snack lunch, a meal for a king comprising a Banon cheese, a handful of olives and a piece of girdle cake; or sitting at the edge of a market in front of a mauresque, a sophisticated mixture of orgeat syrup and pastis, or yet again in the shade of the evening, curved over a farm's sink, a soft soap in one's hand, with the nose prickled by the perfumes of lavender, the ears full of the humming of the crickets, Provence appeals first of all to the senses, and after that to the conscience. This book is not meant to be an exhaustive guide, a simple list of beautiful sites and superb abbeys. It is meant to be a journey through the heart of Provence, both dreamt of and lived in, one of these awakening dreams which this country evokes for today's traveller. This Provence is a country both for the spirit and for the eyes, ethnological inevitably, oenological for the same reason, built by the gentle happiness of a fugitive state of grace, produced by the fatal attention given to contemporary principles.

The little pleasures of Provence

However, there was a time when travellers never stopped here except in exceptional circumstances; particularly the English who used Provence simply as a corridor on their way to Italy, and who pinched their noses at the sight of lands described as wild. But it was this quality of untamed nature which attracted the first "adventurers" seeking a sort of exoticism, almost perverse in their world of coded beauty.

In 1828, Lord and Lady Blessington became pioneers, defying the *Mistral* wind which found its way into even the most comfortable houses, changing tempers and getting on everyone's nerves, responsible for most domestic rows. They went down to the southernmost part of France with three coaches, accompanied by six servants; they saw the fields dotted with wild poppies, the hills blue with lavender, the Roman remains, the roads white with dust, and the whole of this brutal but splendid country.

The little train which went from Orange to Vaison-la-Romaine, for example, took two hours for seventeen miles.

Photo Eric Cattin

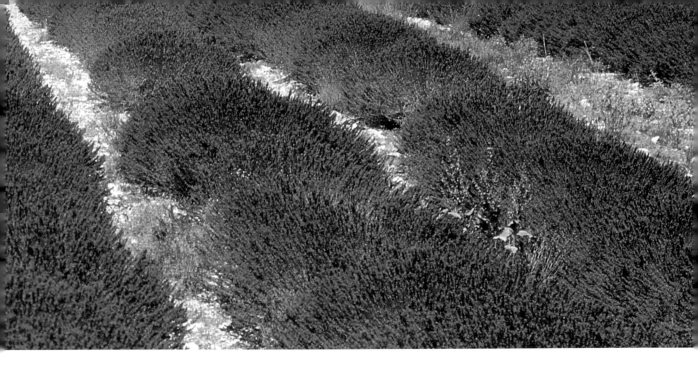

The sun is always the most beautiful the day one sets off

Jean Giono

Tourism was not yet born, travel was slow, three shaky carriages jolted between the hills overlooked by Mont Ventoux. Tired and dirty, one can imagine the pleasure of the first visitors to wash in the waters of a fountain, under a lime tree, waiting for the train to decide to set off again!

Later, Gertrude Stein, great lady of the arts, warned the first rich tourists, the flower of society with Baedecker as their bible, against the hazards of a trip to the Provence country.

Monsieur Beyle himself, better known under the name of Stendhal, and Mérimée too, another great traveller and writer, noted in their diaries the trials of beds shared with strangers in impromptu auberges, their amazement when they saw Aix and Avignon, cities completely forgotten until then in favour of the gentler, more "civilized" Tuscan cities.

Finally, in the splendour of this countryside, one finds the equivalent of what one brings and, at the same time, what one is seeking: oneself, in the innermost recesses of the journey.

In his little book entitled *The ascension of Mont Ventoux*, Petrarch recounts his vision of life through Provence: "To wish for something is little: to acquire it, one has to have the desire (...). When you have wandered a lot, you must climb up towards the summit of beatitude suffering under the weight of a tiresomely deferred fatigue, or else collapse with exhaustion... Thus, drunk with the happiness of the view from this mountain, I turned the eyes of my soul towards myself... Men will admire the mountain peaks, the waves of the Ocean and the movement of the stars, but if they could only forget themselves... "

The quotation from Lao-Tseu which concludes my journey through Provence would not have displeased Petrarch:" The longest journey begins under the sole of your foot".

Market days

Sault : Wednesday morning.
Apt : Saturday morning.
Gordes :Tuesday morning.
Banon : Tuesday morning.
Forcalquier : Monday morning.
Manosque : Saturday morning.
Buis-les-Baronnies : Wednesday and Saturday morning.
Nyons : Wednesday morning and Sunday morning, from June to September.

The route of **Romanesque**
art and silence

ROMANESQUE PROVENCE

The main characteristic of the beginning of Romanesque art is its sobriety. The second age (XIIth, XIIIth centuries) determined the broad outlines of Provençal Romanesque: a simple plan and a desire for severity, a single nave with barrel vaulting, semicircular arches, rare openings, porches with classical decoration. Between 1125 and 1225, the Romanesque influence

Left page:
*The cloister of Saint-Sauveur
(at Aix-en-Provence),
serenity and contemplation.*

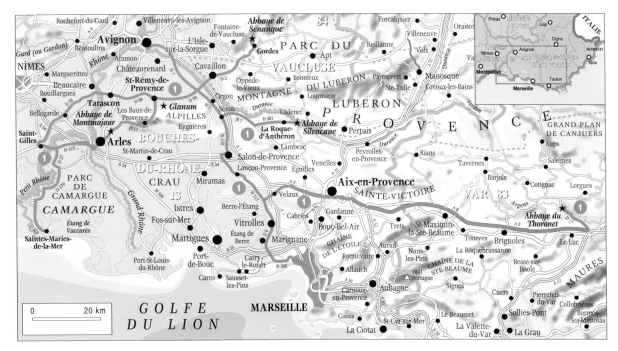

Architecture and spirituality

The term "monk" is used to describe a person who lives apart from the rest of humanity, and who devotes his life to the search for God. There are two possible meanings of the word, whose etymology comes from the Greek monakos, derived from monos. The first, simple and immediate meaning, is alone, solitary. One talked about monks in the case of hermits (eremos, desert) and anchorites (anachoreo), I keep at a distance); only later was the word monk used for men living in monasteries. The second meaning, more rare, is that which describes as monk the unique man, in the sense of unified man.

This second meaning is now taking over from the first in our divided and parted world. We are all submitted to our different roles, and force ourselves to play, one by one, the person who will become mother or father, friend... In these varying roles, we sometimes cannot recognise ourselves.

In monastic life, everything combines to help man to be himself, first of all, before men and before God. This is where

architecture such as Cistercian architecture is interesting: the use of natural materials, simplicity, practicality, authenticity, and this austerity which leaves the structures intact and visible, subliming the beauty of forms through purity.

In contemporary architecture, we are again finding this same search, this voluntary bareness, this same thirst for authenticity, this search for natural materials.

The ideal of the Cîteaux reform was the return of the Rule of Saint Benoît, rectitudo regulae, which stigmatised the superfluous so that man could discover the bounty of the necessary; this search for "less, is more", these days dear to the adepts of the Zen discipline, is found again in nourishment, in clothing, in detachment from material riches, and in the physical and moral satisfaction provided by the study of music, singing, and work well done. The decor of such an internal harmony is that, concise, clear and bare, of Cistercian architecture. The Romanesque is really both art and spirituality!

bequeathed architectural jewels to the département, with Marseilles and Arles as major centres. This was certainly the most productive period for monumental architecture. These edifices, witnesses of a simple and rigorous Provence, austere but refined, built in a measured and serious way, are scattered throughout Provence as places of meditation, spiritual halts where one can retire from one's journey for a short space of time.

This is a route which has to be taken in a studious frame of mind, to savour the very special pleasure of contemplation. It is the route of silence...

A setting of greenery for the harmonious forms of Silvacane Abbey.

Silvacane, La Roque-d'Anthéron

From the left bank of the Durance, one first catches sight of the small blessed belfry, then the light-coloured roofs: the Abbey of Silvacane stands out in all its austerity.

In 1144 the Cistercian order took over the Abbey of Silvacane, one of the three Cistercian "sisters" of Provence, with Le Thoronet and Sénanque. The name Silvacane comes from the Latin *silva cana*, forest of reeds, since the first monks had to fight grimly against the marshy nature which surrounded the first building at that time.

This was not their only fight, since they were expelled from their abbey in 1282 by the monks of Montmajour. They managed to return to Silvacane after a trial, and then followed many years of prosperity, followed by decline, and they finally left the place after the Abbey was annexed to the chapter of the cathedral of Saint-Sauveur d'Aix.

The buildings are arranged around the XIIIth century cloister.

Through its simplicity and the harmony of its proportions, the abbey is one of the most beautiful of Cistercian churches.

Gordes, the Abbey of Notre-Dame de Sénanque

The magic of its lines

Nestled protectively in the hollow of its vale, the Abbey of Notre-Dame de Sénanque is, with Silvacane, and the Thoronet Abbey one of the beauties of Romanesque art in Provence.

Once the summer visitors have gone, the Sénanque Abbey recovers its calm and tranquillity. This is the ideal moment to visit it peacefully. And some days one can have the benefit of a detailed guided visit, accompanied by a lecturer.

The abbey is a sublime witness to early Cistercian architecture, and is now once again inhabited by a community of Cistercian monks. The whole of the XIIIth century edifice is opened to be visited: abbey church,

cloister, dormitory, chapter house, warming room.

The midnight mass at Christmas is the occasion to live a very moving moment at Sénanque, in harmony with the enchantment from these walls. One should also know that the monks receive guests for short spiritual retreats. For information, ask for the brother hotel-keeper. Tel. 04 90 72 05 72.

The cloister of Sénanque Abbey, which through the accomplished simplicity of its architecture illustrates the "rectitudo regulae" so dear to Saint Benoit.

Rigour, strength and silent happiness: Sénanque Abbey welcomes guests for short spiritual retreats.

Sénanque Abbey, in the secret of winter, opens its gates to the faithful on Christmas Eve.

Visit Sénanque

The visit begins with the dormitory. This is a huge chamber with a pointed barrel vault, divided into three unequal parts by two transverse ribs, able to accommodate about thirty monks. The dormitory had no comfort, for this was not allowed in the frugal life of the monasteries: the monks slept on straw mattresses completely clothed. The cornices, at the top of the wall and at the base of the vault, served to support the wooden templates which allowed the vault to be built. A rose window and a window were opened up in the west wall.

Everything in the abbey was organised to encourage prayer and the community liturgy. Thus, for example, the dormitory was built as a direct prolongation of the church transept.

At two o'clock in the morning, the monks left their dormitory for the first church service. In the evening, they went back immediately after the last service.

The abbey church was built in the form of a cross. There is a big apse, lit by three openings which are directed towards the altar, flanked by two apsidal chapels, one on each side, in the pure Romanesque style. Each chapel was used for the celebration of private masses, particularly for the peace of the soul of a benefactor. Above, at the crossing of the transept, the vault rose in the form of a cupola, resting on four pendentives: four small vaults in half-domes, in the form of an arch with six lobes, making it possible to pass from the square shape of the transept crossing to the octagon of the apex of the cupola.

One should walk down the nave and sit at one end to appreciate the church as a whole, typically Cistercian through its extreme austerity.

The rules about decoration were extremely simple: nothing should trouble the prayer and the meditation of the monks. Only light, the symbol of God, punctuates the space.

The monks in the choir occupied the stalls whereas the lay brothers stayed in the part which has benches today. The lay brothers entered the church by side doors at the back. Note the absence of a main porch, which is very rare.

Upon leaving the church, one comes into the cloister. This is the centre of the abbey, a crossing point linking the different parts of the monastery, but above all a place for meditation and reading. Near the door to the church, there is the old armarium where the manuscripts were kept.

The cloister is an inner courtyard, bordered by four galleries opening onto the garden through twelve semi-circular arcades. Here, also, austerity reigns. The capitals of the columns, all different, are decorated simply with vegetal motifs. From the southern gallery, one can see the church belfry and the flat stone roofs, dry stones assembled without a roof frame. A fountain, whose vault toothing can be seen in the south-west angle, was destroyed at the time of the Wars of Religion.

The monks came to work in the calefactory, or warming room. It acted as scriptorium, the place where they copied manuscripts, and was the only heated chamber in the monastery. This small room vaulted with four groined vaults resting in the centre on a strong column with a capital decorated with aquatic leaves and lily flowers, has a very fine conical chimney, able to burn logs placed vertically.

In the chapter house, the monastic community met around the Abbot. There, one read out the Saint Benôit Rule, proceeded with the taking of the habit, and the election of the Father Abbot. The monks sat on tiers of seats and the Father Abbot, placed in the centre, faced the Tarasque, a devil figure sculpted in the cloister. This chamber has wonderful acoustics: the sounds carry thanks to the six intersecting ribs. It was also the only room where the monks were allowed to talk.

Le Thoronet

Together with its sisters of Sivacane and Sénanque, Thoronet Abbey is always cited amongst the marvels of Provence.

It was in 1136 that a group of monks left the Abbey of Mazan in Ardèche to found a monastery on the Tourtour lands.

Then, fifteen years later, they again left their main residence to erect a building about twelve miles away, near Lorgue, which became Thoronet Abbey. The new surroundings were idyllic, with woods and a spring. The work began in 1160 and carried on until 1190.

At the beginning of the XIIIth century, the monastery sheltered about twenty monks and several dozen lay brothers.

But, less than two centuries later, the Abbey started to decline. In 1660, the Prior stated that it was "necessary for the buildings of this abbey to be repaired, since they are in a pitiful condition". The edifice was collapsing, the roofs falling in, and doors and windows deteriorating. However, in 1790, seven monks still resided there.

It was the writer Prosper Mérimée who fell in love with it and saved it by mentioning it to Revoil the architect of

*Le Thoronet is called one of the three Cistercian sisters, with Sénanque and Silvacane Abbeys.
It follows the order's architectural rules which sought ultimate harmony between man and the divine.*

The cloister of Thoronet Abbey, solid and square,

historic monuments. The renovation work began in 1873, and is still continuing regularly today.

Made for prayer and meditation, Romanesque art spread out along the routes of Provence. The central nave of Thoronet Abbey (top left). Tympanum of the Saint-Michel church at Salon-de-Provence (top right). Cloister of the Saint-Sauveur cathedral at Aix (below).

Avignon

In 1039 the monks from Notre-Dame-des-Doms founded the Saint-Ruf Abbey outside the ramparts of the town. Unfortunately, nothing remains of this abbey apart from the belfry, the apse and the transept. Like many other examples of Romanesque art, this also has suffered from ageing... and from men, for the transformations which the abbey underwent during the centuries can only leave one to imagine its former beauty...

Salon-de-Provence

The Saint-Michel church built in the XIIIth century marks a transition. However, a porch from the XIIth remains. A fine Romanesque belfry with arcades dominates the building.

Aix-en-Provence

The Saint-Sauveur cathedral (V[th] to XVIIth centuries) has conserved a Romanesque nave just to the south of the main nave of the elegant XIth century cloister.

Saint-Rémy-de-Provence

In the monastery of Saint-Paul-de-

The old Sainte-Marthe church at Tarascon, which was a collegiate church between the XIIth and XIIIth centuries.

Mausole, one can still visit the cloister and the little church. There is a convalescent home here now, and it is very moving to find within these walls an atmosphere which one can guess is very similar to that, serene despite torments, where Van Gogh had several remissions from his illness. Even though it seems a little strange to see Japanese visitors leaning out from the windows opening onto the cloister, on a calm day it is quite possible to imagine Vincent Van Gogh, silent and methodical, absorbed by a simple painting representing blue irises.

At that time, Van Gogh was considered as a dreamer, with attacks of madness, but not dangerous. He was allowed to paint, both inside and outside; however he was always accompanied by a guardian when he went out. These days, the institute still offers a refuge for fragile persons, treated with therapies which use painting as one of their exercises.

There is a collection of Romanesque chapels on this Provençal route, all with their moving simplicity and sobriety. Among the most remarkable, at **Tarascon**, the old Sainte-Marthe church built as a colle-

Floral motifs and troubling faces, details from the Saint-Paul cloister.

Left: *The cloisters of Saint-Paul de Mausole, at Saint-Rémy, where the worried shadow of Van Gogh wanders.*

17

A facet of the ancient world can be found in the Saint-Gabriel chapel near Tarascon. Here, time stands still.

Montmajour Abbey, solitary queen of Provençal Romanesque.

giate church in the XIIth to XIIIth centuries and the Saint-Gabriel chapel, with its façade inspired by classical antiquity.

The **Montmajour** Abbey is one of the most representative of Provençal Romanesque buildings. It stands on its limestone promontory like a solitary queen, an assembly of light-coloured stone on a ridge, an edifice with refined forms which catches the eye from afar. The abbey of Montmajour emerges from gentle natural surroundings, with swaying grasses, marshy in earlier times.

The abbey was founded in the Xth century by a group of monks, organised as a community. They were not discouraged by the enormity of the task, and began to dry out the surrounding marshes by digging canals and ditches with picks, to drain the plain.

In 1030, the long-awaited land funds arrived; and offerings collected during the Pardon feast, which was instituted at this epoch, helped the pious community to assert itself and become one of the most important religious centres of Provence.

But the spiritual momentum was broken by such abundance: in fact, the

prosperity of the abbey provoked envy. Montmajour was ceded to abbots who made enormous benefits from it, but who abandoned both its appearance and that which had until then supported it: faith.

During the Revolution, the abbey was closed, emptied and sold. Nothing remains now apart from its sumptuous lines, of such purity and charm that they still fascinate, even after centuries of abandon.

The paving of the cloister of Montmajour Abbey shows traces of the steps of praying.

Below, left:
Deep shade and bright light in the chapel of Saint Pierre de Montmajour.
Below:
The little Sainte-Croix chapel at Montmajour: only the birds still sing here...

Arles

The cathedral of Arles is certainly one of the jewels of Romanesque art, dedicated to Saint Trophim in the XIIth century. Pilgrims on their way to Saint-Jacques-de-Compostelle stopped in silence in the cloister, resting in the shade of its vaulting, before continuing on their long journey.

Its cloister is one of the most famous in Provence because of the richness of its sculpted decors and its elegance.

Saint-Trophime at Arles.
Pilgrims on their way
to Saint-Jacques-de-Compostelle
used to rest in this church.

Details from the portal.

Saint-Gilles-du-Gard

There is an attractive legend about the history of the abbey church of Saint-Gilles. It tells how a certain man coming from Athens, where he had lived as a saintly man and had given away all his possessions, arrived in Provence, poor and alone; with a deer for company he lived in a cave where the land was flat. One day his deer was chased by the dogs of the king of the Wisigoths, Wamba. The hunters arrived at the cave, and found the dogs lying at the feet of the saint. The king was so impressed that he gave Saint Gilles the funds to build the abbey.

What remains of this edifice are the magnificent façade, with three porches, the ruins of the choir and the splendid spiral staircase from the northern belfry, carved in stone.

The façade of Saint-Gilles-du-Gard with its three portals. Little remains of this church which has not been spared by the centuries.

The apostles around Christ, details from the portal.

Nearby, the Romanesque Saint-Laurent church, with its xvii[th] century belfry, dominates the Saint-Jean fort. From the other side of the Old Port, the imposing silhouette of the crenellated towers of the Saint-Victor Abbey faces it; it is one of the most complex monuments of the Bouches-du-Rhône.

The crypts from the xiii[th] century include the ruins of the edifice from the vth century created by Cassien; they form a succession of chapels decorated with stelae and sculptures from the xii[th] to xv[th] centuries. From the xi[th] century, the golden age, there remains the "Isarn Porch". The tall church, built in the xiii[th] century, very sober, is a fine example of Provençal Romanesque, despite the late date of its creation. The fortifications are from the xiv[th] century.

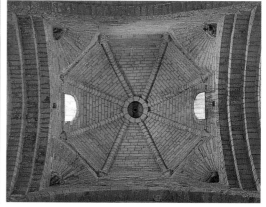

In the Saint-Victor crypt, at Marseilles, a disturbing face.

The Saint-Laurent church at Marseilles dominates the Saint-Jean fort.

It is said that the Devil and the Good Lord can be recognised from details... Above, the cupola of the Old Major cathedral, and goat's ears for this stone head, in the chapel of Saintes-Maries-de-la-Mer.

Saintes-Maries-de-la-Mer

In Camargue, at Saintes-Maries-de-la-Mer, the church of Notre-Dame-de-la-Mer was built in the xii[th] century. Fortifications covered the Romanesque façade during the Hundred Years' War. Inside there are some remarkable capitals decorated with vegetal carvings and human figures.

Marscilles

Around 1150, on the site of a previous edifice next to a huge baptistery a cathedral in a very austere Romanesque style was built: "the Old Major".

Today, after the alterations and mutilations carried out to build the present cathedral, there only remains a vast nave and an octagonal cupola.

The art of gardens

The search for beauty and serenity – but also a certain sensuality – exudes from every artistic creation in this region, which has been especially indulged by the gods.

Gardens and their creation accompanied the building of the most beautiful abbeys and contributed to their subtle enchantment, involving body and spirit. There is, of course, the pleasure of the eyes, but also shade, perfumes, the incessant changing of the seasons, with their philosophical meaning and their profound and natural significance. However, the gardens of this region have remained little known, partly because many are private and partly because, contrary to those of England or the Ile-de-France, they have never separated the useful from the agreeable, profit from pleasure. The Provençal garden has never renounced its agricultural roots. It is a balance between the values of the land and the refinement of visual harmonies, rural architectures and the garden which is also a vegetable garden, a store of rare essences, the edge of a shrubbery...

The culture which gave birth to the concept of the Provençal garden dates back to Roman times.

The Romans were the first to design the landscapes of the South, with agricultural lands which mixed so well with the hills, the garrigue, and the gentle plains. In Tuscany, the Romans had already civilised the land, transforming it into huge agricultural domains, planted with vineyards and orchards, uniting the two axes of utility and productivity.

In the same way, certain mas of the Alpilles, surrounded by cultivated land, trees and bordered paths, have foundations dating back to the time of Christ. The land was already divided up, almost the same as it is now.

The Romans also had the art of giving diverse shapes to evergreen plants - topiaries, which are so much in fashion these days. They also knew how to make shade and let the sun shine in depending on the seasons, they planted hedges against the north wind and managed water supplies. The general lines are still laid out by hedges, box, laurels, evergreen oak, myrtle and rosemary.

One of the other important elements of the gardens of Provence is stone, in the form of arches, small walls, statues. The first travellers were captivated by this, and their travel diaries are full of water-colour paintings and charcoal sketches representing the light and shade of the moving foliage, the bright tones of the flowers, and these more solid contours which limit the spaces.

These days, summer flowerings are the most in demand. According to the tourist image, Provence is as it is seen on postcards, highly coloured like the ochre houses of certain villages or like the famous Provençal fabrics. But, even now, for the experienced eye of a traveller who does not stop at the surface of what is visible, there is another truth, preserved in the niches of its habitat: one has to know how to look at it.

The Barben gardens near Salon-de-Provence, designed by Le Nôtre. A clever integration of the artificial into the natural habitat.

A stroke of the brush

In present representations of Provence, the olive tree and the cypress, these two trees which are so representative of the Mediterranean world are often married together: but cypresses have only been part of the Provençal landscape since relatively recent times... Thus, when Van Gogh arrived in Provence, in 1888, they had only been there for one generation.

Grey stone and tiles: Les Baux-de-Provence fit perfectly into the Provençal landscape.

Moving simplicity of the remains of the Saint-Sixte chapel, at Eygalières.

It would be pretentious to believe that all the Romanesque monuments can be cited, since Provence is overflowing with them, at a bend, or glimpsed at the side of the road, jewels which are sometimes less well preserved than the magnificent abbeys which are very visited, very well known. Sometimes, the Romanesque of these churches is mixed with other styles or quite simply has been modified over the years. The following have several moving arcades, several light and square belfries for a more adventurous day, a more relaxed search: Notre-Dame-du-Château at

Saint-Etienne-du-Grès, built on a rocky spur. The church of Sainte-Baudile de Noves: a Romanesque nave with four bays. The Saint-Jean-du-Grès chapel at Fontvielle, deliberately austere. The Saint-Sixte chapel at Eygaliers. The Saint-Blaise chapel and Saint-Vincent church, XIIth century, half troglodyte, at the Baux-de-Provence. The Saint-Cyr chapel of Lançon, near the old cemetery. The Notre-Dame-de-la-Pitié chapel at Maussane.

Solid and well-built, the chapel of Saint-Cyr de Lançon stands near the old cemetery.

The artists' route

Avignon
Saint-Rémy-de-Provence
Arles
Martigues
L'Estaque
Marseille
Aix

The most important artists of the last century worked on a sun-drenched route. From Avignon to Arles in the steps of Van Gogh, from the port of l'Estaque to Marseilles following the tracks of Cézanne, these stony paths, these routes whitened with dust, immobile under skies heavy with heat or imprisoned by the polished blue of the *Mistral*, meant that Provence was never the same again after the passage of these painters. From about 1850, until 1920, landscapes and places changed, fashions faded and wars were declared; and this generous Provence, the chosen land for nature and avant-garde painters, impartial host to the fauvists, the impressionists and the cubists, gave refuge to the most wise talents and the most wild. This route which winds between hedges of honeysuckle and saffron coloured reeds, which twists around a square-shaped belfry, and then serpents among the bent olive trees in infinite fields, this route, invisible and dreamt of, is also the route of light which, under the artist's paint brush, changes incessantly...

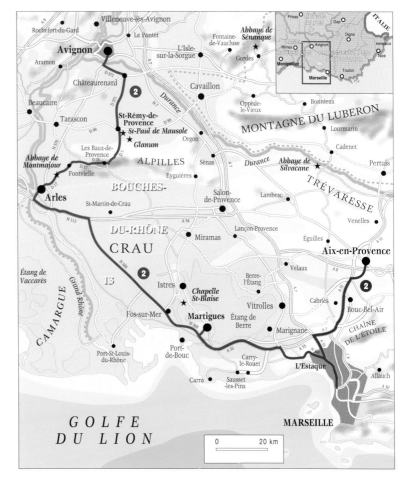

Paul Cézanne. Still Life. Sugar bowl, pears and a blue cup. Circa 1865. Granet Museum, Palais de Malte, Aix-en-Provence. *Photo: Bernard Terlay.*

Avignon

The first Pope to settle in Avignon was Clement V. Then the period of splendours began... Above, the bridge of Avignon and below, the Popes' Palace.

There is no doubt that the history of Avignon dates back to the earliest times of Antiquity. It is certain that the Rocher-des-Doms, emerging from the waters of the Rhône, was frequented by Prehistoric man, even though it is impossible to put a date to the first human settlement.

The site was inhabited in 4,000 years B.C. by the Chassey culture peoples who practised cattle breeding and agriculture, and whose civilisation extended from central Italy to Burgundy.

From 500 B.C. the town extended considerably around the oppidum built on the Rocher. It was occupied by the Cavares Celtic-Ligurian peoples.

The name of the town dates from this epoch. "Aouen (n) ion", a name of Cavare origin but with two interpretations: "the town of high winds" or "master of the river", depending on whether the translation is based on the Celtic or the Ligurian.

In any case, the destiny of Avignon changed at the beginning of the XIVth century, when it began to take on the appearance which we know today: the exile of the Pontifical Court to France marks the century which really created Avignon. This was its period of splendour. The first Pope to decide to reside in France was Clement V, and he chose the Comtat Venaissin which the Holy See had owned since 1247. He died in 1314, and in 1316 an ageing pope, John XXII, succeeded him. He resided in the Episcopal Palace situated to the south of the cathedral. His successors, Benedict XII and especially Clement VI, who bought Avignon from Queen Joan of Sicily for 80,000 florins, installed the papacy in the appropriate luxury, thus making Avignon the most envied court in Europe for artists, monks, tradesmen and pilgrims.

"After passing Pont-Saint-Esprit, a sharp bend revealed the arches of the famous bridge, broken and abandoned in the middle of the river (...) Behind these walls stood the rigid mass of the Popes' Palace, above a tangle of roofs in red tiles" (James Pope-Hennessy).

Avignon, lozenge shaped, traced out by the bends of the Rhône, sheltered by its ramparts, is a city which leaves no one indifferent.

Mérimée, Mistral and Dickens described it with words filled with the powerful wind and sheer blue of the sky, entire generations of artists, both local and from abroad, fell under its charm, making a puzzle of shapes and colours of the city, in which the eye often loses itself.

The names of these painters are often known only to their followers, and yet their vision of the town is present in the eyes of those looking for the other face, less evident, that of a second and deeper regard.

The famous artist at the national level is the landscape painter Paul Saïn, but it is Pierre Grivolas, close to the Félibriges (XIXth century society aimed at preserving the Provençal language), witness of this movement of regional identity inspired by Frédéric Mistral, who probably reflected best the powerful state of mind.

The Félibriges

Tradition has it that six young Provençal poets (Joseph Roumanille, Théodore Aubanel, Jean Brunet, Paul Giera, Anselme Mathieu, Alphonse Tavan), grouped around Frédéric Mistral, founded the Félibrige movement on March 21st 1854 in the Font-Ségugne château in the Vaucluse.

The word "félibre" has been given several explanations, some of which have been accepted. Frédéric Mistral himself was perfectly happy to let doubt reign, sometimes admitting that he borrowed the name from a cantilena which was recited formerly at Maillane, the Prayer to Saint Anselm:

La quatrièimo doulour
 qu'ai souferto pèr vous,
 O moun fiéu tant precious,
 Es quand vous perdeguère,
 Que de tres jour, tres
  niue, iéu noun vous
  retrouvère,
 Que dins lou tèmple erias,
 Que vous disputavias
 Emé li tiroun de la Lèi,
 Emé li sèt félibre de la
  Lèi.

Other hypotheses link the etymology with the low Latin fellebris, which means pupil, or disciple. The fact cannot be excluded that, knowing the love and the close relation between Mistral and the resonance of words, he could have adopted this because of its lightness, its claws like a young cat, and its very volatile meaning... In any case this is one of the reasons why writers in love with Provence found a choice in félibres, free felines, free nymphs...

Director of the Fine Arts School of Avignon from 1878 to 1905, he was such a rebel and visionary that he was able to attract his pupils from the surrounding academies. With a sense of freedom and colour touching that of the impressionists, he passed on to his disciples the taste and desire to confront landscapes in the open air and the light.

The best known among his painters are Claude Firmin and Victor Leydet, excellent observers of day-to-day life. Others, less well known, such as Eugène Martel, Marius Roux-Renard, Clément Brun, Alfred Lesbros, are interesting and one can admire their works in the town museums.

Following in the footsteps of the painters: the light and shade of Avignon

Vieux-Sextier Street

Pierre Grivolas often painted this street, one of the most beautiful in the city, at the heart of Avignon. This walk which starts from the Sextier to reach Pie Square was built in 1479. L'Hôtel de Belli, at the angle of the Fourbisseurs street, is one of the oldest houses in Avignon.

Pie Square

The vegetable market which was held on this square, and which was closed at the beginning of the xx[th] century, was one of the subjects which Clément Brun and Grivolas liked to treat. Their easels were often to be seen placed in a corner of these market halls, the first dating back to 1563. As for the present market, it dates from 1899 and was modernised several times. A little further on, there is a pretty flower market which is still in action.

Barthelasse Isle

Many pictures have been painted of the shores of the isle; the best known is probably by Paul Saïn, *"November Twilight"*, which can be seen in the Calvet museum.

From this isle – whose name comes from the Provençal *bartalasso*, or brushwood – the view of Avignon is so beautiful that at dusk even these days many stay there a while, with an easel or even with empty hands...

In the Calvet museum and the Roure Palace one can find the same view, looked at a thousand times but never in the same way, on numerous paintings and engravings.

The Avignon museums: full of canvasses

The Calvet Museum, 65 rue Joseph-Vernet, tel. 04 90 86 33 84. A splendid house from the xviii[th] century, with its paved main courtyard and gardens. An encyclopaedic museum, Prehistoric, Egyptian, Greek, Roman collections, and paintings from the xvi[th] to xx[th] century, as well as works by Grivolas, Bonnard, Manet, Guigou, Dufy, Leydet, Chabaud, Manguin and Vlaminck.

The Petit-Palais Museum, Palace Square, tel. 04 90 44 58 86. Italian Primitive paintings (end xiii[th] - beginning xv[th] centuries), Romanesque sculptures and xv[th] century paintings from the Avignon school.

Roure Palace, 3 rue-du-Roure, tel. 04 90 80 80 88. The meeting point for the Mistral language. Museum of Provençal traditions and folklore, grouping together the works of Grivolas, Roux-Renard and Flour.

And also:

The Aubanel Museum, Saint-Pierre Square, tel. 04 90 86 35 02. Aubanel, a dramatic author from Avignon was one of the founders of the Félibrige (xix[th] century). The history of the Félibrige and Provençal literature.

Saint-Rémy-de-Provence

It is impossible to pass by Saint-Rémy without thinking of its most famous and most unhappy painter, without thinking of the tragedy of his life... and also without seeing the olive trees in the surrounding countryside, the landscapes, the flowers, through the eyes of Van Gogh. Even unconsciously, his visions are superposed on the charming and vivacious town which one visits today.

Paul Cézanne. Still life with an earthenware pot. © Angladon / C. Loury.

An exceptional museum

The Angladon museum at 5, rue du Laboureur, tel. 04 90 82 29 03. This is a place of extraordinary charm gathering together some of the most interesting works of our epoch, collected by the famous Parisian couturier Jacques Doucet.

This museum displays paintings by Van Gogh, Picasso, Cézanne, Manet, and also Degas, Monet, Daumier, Vuillard, Derain, Foujita, Modigliani, Sisley. On the ground floor, for example, one can see Railway wagons by Van Gogh and Still Life with an earthenware pot by Cézanne.

This latter painting corresponds to a decisive moment in the manner the master painted. After his years of youth, he finally achieved a plastic mastery of the subjects he researched with.

As for Railway wagons, painted in Arles in 1888, it is the only painting by the artist to be found in a museum in Provence. In a letter to his brother Théo, Van Gogh refers to an "itinerant stop, with red and green carriages", corresponding today to the famous painting in the Orsay Museum in Paris and this "little study of carriages on the Paris-Lyons-Mediterranean" line.

The visit ends with XVIIth century salons, a Far-East salon, paintings and drawings, signed furniture, objets d'art. There is a medieval and Renaissance hall and a XVIIth century salon.

Vincent Van Gogh. Railway carriages. © Angladon / C. Loury.

Vincent Van Gogh, portrait of the artist, 1889.
Paris, Musée d'Orsay.

Vincent Van Gogh

He was born in the Dutch province of Brabant, in 1853, a year to the day after the birth and death of a little brother, Vincent; his parents gave him the name of his dead brother. The elder son of a pastor, agitated by interior troubles which he attributed to a mystic vocation, Van Gogh began to draw very early.

However, he only gave himself completely to painting when he was twenty-seven. He went to Brussels where he followed brief academic studies, and then he studied under the direction of a relative, the painter Anton Mauve. He admired Millet and Israels, and painted in their manner; like them, he showed the life of workers, the miners of the Borinage, poor people and those who frequented hospices.

The Potato Eaters, a canvas dating from 1885, was painted in the Millet style, and is probably his most important work from this period impregnated by religious fervour.

In February 1886, in Paris, he finally discovered the impressionists and saw the works of Camille Corot and Honoré Daumier in the Goupil Gallery where his brother Théo worked. Henri de Toulouse-Lautrec painted his portrait, Camille Pissaro explained Pointillism to him, father Tanguy, owner of an art shop, gave him canvasses in exchange for his work, and he met Edgar Degas, Georges Seurat, Paul Signac and Paul Gauguin. It was through his contact with these artists and his long visits to the Louvre museum where he spent entire days, that Vincent Van Gogh with the constant and solid support of his brother Théo, began to paint still life and landscapes in the style of the pointillists and neo-impressionists.

He then left Paris, a city in which he had learnt a great deal but which had a bad effect on his health, in February 1888.

In Provence, at Arles, he fell in love with the lights and the colours, and worked "like a madman", eating when he remembered, and living alone and poor.

Midday
or the Siesta, 1890.
Paris, Musée d'Orsay.

Corn-field, 1889.
Amsterdam, Rijksmuseum Vincent Van Gogh.

It was at this moment that his painting became radiant, his lines simple and powerful, his moods violent and demanding.

He painted The Night Café, and various designs similar to Japanese engravings, which he had discovered and studied during a stay at Antwerp.

In September 1888, he settled in the "Yellow House" in Arles, after deciding that Gauguin should join him there to begin to found a sort of artists' colony. Gauguin left Brittany and joined him in October, but he didn't like the country. Gauguin soon started to think about returning to the north. This decision hurt Van Gogh profoundly, since he was already upset by the announcement of his brother Théo's engagement to be married.

On Christmas Eve of the same year, 1888, he had his first attack of madness. It was during this night that Vincent Van Gogh cut off his own ear to offer it to the prostitutes in the nearby brothel. He was taken to hospital and remained unconscious for three days.

He decided himself to go into the asylum at Saint-Rémy, so as not to be a burden on Théo, who had just married. Periods of lucidity alterna-

Fishing boats on the beach, 1888. *Amsterdam, Rijksmuseum Vincent Van Gogh.*

ted with times of madness, but he continued to work with all his strength. The cypress is the persistent representation of this part of the life of Van Gogh.

In May, he left Saint-Rémy, to make a short visit to Paris to see Théo and his family, then he left for Auvers-sur Oise, as the guest of Doctor Gachet.

In the gentle light of the Île-de-France, he painted magnificent fields of corn, and seemed to rediscover a certain serenity. But the crows' shadows were overhead, and news of his brother's departure for Holland plunged him into new anguish.

On July 27th, Vincent Van Gogh put an end to his sufferings, to his unique painting and to his visions: in yet another of his deliriums, he wounded himself in the chest with a revolver.

Théo was called, and came from Paris, but could only witness the last hours of torment of his well-loved brother: on July 29th 1890, Van Gogh died.

Van Gogh's house at Arles, the Yellow House, 1888.
Amsterdam, Rijksmuseum Vincent Van Gogh.

The cloister of Saint-Paul de Mausole, in the footsteps of Van Gogh.

The town, born after the destruction of Glanum, surrounded by the Alpilles, full of flowers, shaded by plane trees and decorated with fountains, grew under the protection of the Saint-Rémy Abbey in Rheims, thus the present name of the town.

A circuit called "Walks through the places painted by Vincent Van Gogh" takes visitors to the artist's favourite sites.

In the footsteps of Van Gogh

Monastery of Saint-Paul de Mausole

This old monastery has preserved a very pretty cloister and a Romanesque Provençal belfry. In the alley a bronze bust by Zadkine represents a painter at work. The travel-writer James Pope-Hennessy described these places, attributing the bust in stone to "some old pensioner with talent" in the first version of his book *Aspects of Provence*, and to a local sculptor called

Bust of Vincent Van Gogh.

Thoret in the version dated 1964. According to this sculptor, it was a "degenerated gatherer of Italian mimosa in the mountains of the Esterel".

It is strange to note how sometimes, from book to work to travel guide, errors are repeated and how difficult it often is to know the real truth

34

about a painting, an example of architecture, a legend. Perhaps, finally, a country is understood more intimately this way, with a mixture of true and false which adjusts to the vision of each...

Les Antiques - Glanum

The Roman civilisation left two magnificent examples of its architecture on French soil, at Saint-Rémy, or rather in the old city of Glanum: the triumphal arch and the Julius mausoleum.

They count amongst the best known monuments in France, without any doubt.

Before entering the excavations, from high up one finds one of the views

Les Antiques at Saint-Rémy, two monuments which have always attracted many visitors. Below: the ruins of the ancient town of Glanum.

In the Alpilles, the place called "Van Gogh's Spectacles".

The obsessions of Van Gogh

The vast olive groves around Saint-Rémy, with their Burnt Sienna land and their shivering silver leaves, was one of the preferred subjects for Van Gogh. The black of the knotted tree trunks and the swaying pale green were painted in series, first of all in June and July, then at harvest time, in November 1889, just before his death.

which inspired Van Gogh to create his works *The Two Holes* and the *Saint-Rémy Mountain*, painted in July 1889. He also painted the Glanum quarry several times.

L'Hôtel d'Estrine, tel. 04 90 92 34 72, a fine dwelling from the XVIIIth century, shelters an art centre, Présence Van Gogh, and holds thematic exhibitions about the artist

Arles

"Nature is extraordinarily beautiful here. Everything is perfect, the dome of the sky is an admirable blue, and the sun shines like pale sulphur" (Vincent Van Gogh).

If Van Gogh left his glowing mark at Saint-Rémy, in Arles his hand adapted to a beauty and power more brutal, more sumptuous.

The narrow ridges, the mineral universe, the far-off mountains and this special light inspired other painters apart from Van Gogh, among whom one can cite J.-R. Isnard and the American Mac Knight. Unfortunately for these good artists, the presence of Van Gogh overwhelmed any other style of painting...

His Arlesian period dated from the 21st February 1888 to the 3rd May 1889, and his paintings reflect a concentration and minimalism close to Japanese prints. One can also see traces of the influence of Gauguin, one of the painters Van Gogh admired the most, even if their friendship came to an unhappy end the evening when Vincent, in the throes of his illness, tried to attack Gauguin and then finally cut off his own ear.

Arles in paintings

Forum Square

If one looks for the "Night Café" where Van Gogh painted one of his "Starry Nights", one may well be disappointed. But Forum Square still exists, an animated centre, bordered with cafés, in the busy heart of the town centre.

Vincent Van Gogh. The Olive Grove, 1889, Amsterdam, Rijksmuseum.

The dishevelled charm of silvery plains.

The Alyscamps at Arles,
a wonderfully lyrical spot.

The arenas

Probably built towards the end of the Ist century or right at the beginning of the IInd, at the Flavian epoch, the arenas only appear on one of the canvasses of Van Gogh, who only painted ancient monuments in distant silhouette.

The Alyscamps

This site, which inspired poets so much, with its romantic ruins and forgotten tombs, was discovered by Van Gogh only when Gauguin visited it. In a way, he thus saw this "Champs-Elysées" through the eyes of his friend. In one week, he painted it four times.

From Gauguin, one can see the Alyscamps on a canvas exhibited in the Orsay Museum in Paris.

Arles, amphitheatre.

The Trinquetaille bridge

This bridge was almost completely destroyed by the bombing of 1944. One can see how it looked on one the canvasses of Van Gogh.

Espace Van Gogh

This hospital sheltered Van Gogh after his crisis of December 24th 1889. The former hospital and garden were restored following the painting left by the artist.

The Arles Museums

The Réattu Museum, 10 rue du Grand-Prieuré, tel. 04 90 49 36 74. Installed in the former Maltese priory, this magnificent museum holds works from the XVIIth and XVIIIth centuries from the Arlesian studios. In May 1971, Picasso offered thirty-one sketches of the town, which are on show in the museum.

The Van Gogh Foundation, 24 bis, rond-point des Arènes, tel. 04 90 49 94 04. In homage to Van Gogh, exhibitions of painting and study circuits are organised.

Martigues

In this little port which was one of the preferred sites of Dufy, Picabia and Ziem, it is difficult to discover the charm which inspired their paintings.

The historic centre has managed to keep a trace, but unfortunately all the factories around have suffocated the spirit.

Nevertheless, with a bit of imagination, one can still look at this old fishing port in the sun as seen by

The L'Anglois Bridge at Arles.

enthusiasts such as the Marseillais Jean-Baptiste Olive, Alfred Casile, Charles Pellegrin, Joseph Garibaldi – not to be confused with his Italian homonym – Raymond Allègre and Théophile Decanis. But the artist one thinks of first of all remains Ziem: an exile of Armenian and Polish origin, who opened a studio on the banks of the Caronte canal. His work anticipated that of the impressionists and makes one think of Manet.

Sites, water, colours...

The Berre Lagoon

The port of Martigues is anchored here, and the white façades of the houses correspond to the light-coloured sails in the water. In the Ziem museum, one can see a Picabia painted in 1905, representing the Berre lagoon.

The Saint-Sébastien canal and the Sainte-Madeleine church, at Martigues, have a little old-world feel.

*The Brescon canal
or "birds' mirror"*

This is a charming stretch of water, surrounded by the coloured houses of fishermen, and was one of the preferred sites of artists.

The Ziem Museum, Boulevard du 14-Juillet, tel. 04 42 80 66 06. This museum, installed in the former XIXth century customs barracks, contains many works by Ziem, but also by Brest, Manguin and Picabia.

L'Estaque

"I have rented a little house in l'Estaque, just above the station... At sunset, if one climbs higher, there is a superb panorama of Marseilles and the isles, all enveloped very decoratively in the evening..." (Paul Cézanne to his friend Emile Zola).

" Nothing can equal the majesty of these gorges which dig deep between the hills, the narrow paths winding down to the bottom of a ravine, the arid flanks planted with pine-trees, erecting walls the colours of rust and blood." (Emile Zola).

L'Estaque is now an intimate part of Marseilles life, but there was a time when it regularly received guests such as Cézanne, Braque, Derain, Dufy and Marquet. Impressionists, Fauvists and Cubists were also closely linked to the life of this old popular quarter. A small and picturesque fishing port, sheltered from all the winds, l'Esteque became an industrial suburb at the end of the XXth century; chemistry and cement brought in jobs but also problems.

L'Estaque. Photo G. Detaille.

These days, the beach is not next to l'Estaque, separated from the sea by several ranks of dikes. The factories have closed, and so the village should become a very agreeable residential quarter. In the winter sun or in the shade of the plane trees, many inhabitants of Marseilles invade the restaurant terraces on the edge of the port." But l'Estaque does not only have this outlet to the sea. The village, huddled against the mountains, is crossed by paths which lose themselves in the middle of a confusion of stricken rocks. The Marseilles-Lyons railway runs between huge blocks of stone, crosses ravines over bridges and suddenly enters the rock itself and stays there for a league and a half, in this Nerthe tunnel, the longest in France." (Georges Braque).

Paul Cézanne. Landscape at Caesar's tower, 1862. *Granet Museum, Palais de Malte, Aix-en-Provence. Photo: Bernard Terlay.*

Paul Cézanne. Apotheosis of Delacroix. 1890-1894. *Granet Museum, Palais de Malte, Aix-en-Provence. Photo: Bernard Terlay.*

Paul Cézanne

"Chats about art are almost useless" (January 28th 1902).

Paul Cézanne was born in Aix-en-Provence on January 19th 1839. In his lycée, he met Emile Zola, and was a close friend for many years. As children, they roamed around the countryside with a third boy called Baptistin Baille; together they discussed art at length. They also read their respective verses. When Zola left for Paris in 1858, he continued writing to Cézanne.

Little Paul had a strange character, capricious and changing; it was only in 1860 that his feeling for painting drew him towards clumsy copies of works in the museum.

Although, obeying his father, he agreed to study law, he usually forgot to open his books and his father, finally, allowed him to go to Paris to continue his art studies.

Six months later he returned to Aix. He did not appreciate Parisian life, became depressed and spent his days in the Louvre Museum. The experience was not conclusive and, despite the disappointment of Zola, Cézanne returned to Aix intending to begin to work with his father.

But, obviously, nothing could satisfy him. At the end of 1862, Cézanne left again for Paris, his friend Zola and his studio.

Thanks to Pissarro, he met Claude Monet, Frédérique Bazille and Pierre-Auguste Renoir. In the cafes he avoided discussion, since he detested being contradicted, and he became very angry when thwarted. In 1863, he fell in love with the painting "Déjeuner sur l'herbe" by Edouard Manet. In his turn, several years later Manet himself fell in love with the still-lifes of Cézanne. Despite the admiration of the artists who knew him, Cézanne's paintings did not sell well. They even annoyed: one of his canvasses, exhibited in a boutique in Marseilles, created so much anger among the crowd that it had to be withdrawn. When the Franco-Prussian war broke out in 1870, he returned to the South and lived in l'Estaque with Hortense Fiquet, his model, whom he later married. But, in 1872, he deliberately decided to change style. He wanted to learn about the new impressionist manner, with its light touches, its broken up colours and its interest in the play of light.

In 1874, he took part in the first exhibition organised by the impressionist group, and also in the second in 1877. But nothing happened, no success, and money problems became more and more serious. His father discovered his liaison with Hortense and, indignant, reduced his allowance. His friends helped, especially Zola: but the friendship between the two ceased when Zola published L'Œuvre. The sensitive Cézanne detected a link between the hero of the novel, an unsuccessful artist, and himself. The death of his father in 1886 put an end to his problems, since he inherited a small fortune. When his mother died in 1897, her fine house, the Jas de Bouffant, was sold.

On October 15th 1906, while he was painting outside, there was an unexpected storm and he was soaked to the very bones. He had to be take back home, and died on October 22nd.

Nature often inspired the paintings of Cézanne, and his love for nature gave his landscapes this austere, bare vision, almost severe. He went beyond the lyricism of the impressionists to plunge into another reality, epic, profound, monumental.

The rigorous arrangement of his paintings, due to his acute observation, was not imposed by a theoretical or intellectual necessity, but by a penetrating need for order, by a search for existing harmony, that of the universe.

Paul Cézanne. Kiss of the Muse. circa 1860.
Granet Museum, Palais de Malte, Aix-en-Provence.
Photo: Bernard Terlay.

Paul Cézanne. The bathers. circa 1895. Granet Museum, Palais de Malte, Aix-en-Provence. Photo: Bernard Terlay.

Paul Cézanne. Bathsheba. 1885-1890.
Granet Museum, Palais de Malte, Aix-en-Provence. Photo: Bernard Terlay.

Paul Cézanne.
Portrait
of Madame Cézanne.
1885-1887.
Granet Museum, Palais de Malte,
Aix-en-Provence.
Photo: Bernard Terlay.

Paul Cézanne. 1839-1906. Nude with a mirror. Granet Museum, Palais de Malte,
Aix-en-Provence. Photo: Bernard Terlay.

The Old Port at Marseilles which, during hot summer nights, smells of salt and grilled sardines.

L'Estaque in paintings

Church Square

Between 1870 and 1882, Cézanne stayed several times in l'Estaque. He lived in Church Square. In 1870 Zola joined him there for several days.

The Marinier Vale

At the end of the Marinier path, one has to take the footpath leading to a very well preserved site, which appears in the painting called Rocks of l'Estaque.

The port

After Cézanne, Derain often painted the fishing boats in the ports, as well as Braque, Marquet and Friesz.

Riaux Vale

During the summer of 1908, Braque decided to paint a group of houses which can still be seen. *Maisons de l'Estaque*, the title of the painting, marked the beginning of cubism

Marseille

Founded in 600 B.C. by the Phocaeans on the banks of Lake Lacydon, the town of Massalia has always been a cross-roads of ideas, races and civilisations. Marseilles is dazzling, a thousand year old port, a mysterious and secret city, whose inhabitants know the slightest by-ways by magic. It is also the city where the feminine and masculine are Mediterranean, and thus cannot mix. The mythical founder of Marseilles is incarnated in the story of Gyptis, this Ligurian princess who chose Protis, the Phocaean leader the very night he entered the port.

The beauties of this city, sometimes veiled and never evident, have been chosen by generations of painters who have captured the sea mist, the colours of the shore, and the overlapping of shapes in the old quarters. Towards the middle of the XIXth century, under the influence of Loubon who directed the Marseilles design school, a real Provençal school of landscape painters emerged, among the best known Paul Guigou, Adolphe Monticelli, Jean-Baptiste Olive.

After this first wave of naturalist painters came other waves of local or foreign artists, such as Alfred Lombard, Alfred Casile, Pierre Girieux, Raoul Dufy and Albert Marquet. Their works are exhibited in the city museums: and then to search for these contours and these ambiences is a way of understanding Marseilles better, and to deserve these treasures.

Marseilles, step by step...

The Old Port

Verdilhan, Signac and Marquet often painted the former Lacydon, the fine old port of Marseilles, which is now a marina. They liked to draw it from the gardens of the Pharo, at sunset.

The corniche

From the corniche, one can see the islands and the Marseilles roadstead. This avenue which follows the coast for nearly two miles offers superb viewpoints, particularly loved and often reproduced by Jean-Baptiste Olive and Bernard Crémieux.

The Panier

"The N... bar", painted by Alfred Lombard, could be one of the numerous cafes in this bric-à-brac district, one of the most picturesque in Marseilles. One reaches it via the "Montée des Accoules", and from the top one overlooks the port and the Virgin of the Garde.

The Goudes

At the end of the promenade at the edge of the sea, one discovers this unexpected site, away from the beaten track, which Adolphe Moutte loved so much. It is a little fishing port which has kept its picturesque aspect.

Museums in Marseilles

The Cantini museum, 19 rue Grignan, tel. 04 91 54 77 75. Works by Lombard, Dufy, Derain, Picasso, Chagall, Matisse.

The Fine Arts museum, Palais Longchamp, tel. 04 91 62 21 17. In the XIXth century gallery, one finds works by the Provençal landscape painters Olive, Monticelli, Guigou.

The Grobet-Labadié museum, 140 Boulevard Longchamp, tel. 04 91 62 21 82.

Notre-Dame-de-la-Garde, on the hills overlooking the Old Port, protects the city of Marseilles.

The Auffes vale at Marseilles, a fragment of beauty lost in the city.

The Sainte-Victoire mountain, painted many times by a Cézanne in search of the "third dimension".

Built at the end of the last century, this museum was originally the home of a Marseilles merchant. One see works by Ziem, Guigou and Monticelli here...

Aix

Aix was the capital of Provence for many years; this is evident from its architecture, the richness of its town houses, and the traces of its flamboyant past which still exist.

It is a very beautiful town surrounding by a nature which is generous, both protected and dominated by the Sainte-Victoire mountain which culminates at 3316 feet.

When Cézanne settled in Aix, in 1890, the aesthetic debate between the artists of the town grew in amplitude: two camps appeared which, already traditionally antagonists, became frankly enemies – the debate between tradition and modernity. In this battle, Louis Leydet, post-impressionist with romantic sensitivity was followed by Achille Emperaire, Barthélemy Niollon and Joseph Ravaisou. They continued to paint in the anti-academic manner, following a personal research.

As for Cézanne, he did not limit himself to impressionism, but opened the way to a third dimension, which he tried to reproduce by the use of colour.

The Sainte-Victoire mountain became the favourite theme of the painter, and his consecrated subject. It appeared in his work for the first time in 1870, in a painting entitled *La Tranchée*. Between 1885 and 1886, the artist painted it in all its forms, all its nuances. Strangely, only one canvas from this series remains in France.

A Cézanne tour

The Saint-Sauveur cathedral

Cézanne passed in front of this church to reach his studio. He frequented it assiduously at the end of his life.

The Sainte-Victoire

The emblem of Cézanne, the Sainte-Victoire mountain, 7 to 8 miles long and visible from everywhere, still dominates the landscape around Aix. In August 1989 there was a huge fire on its slopes, and 12,500 acres went up in smoke....

The Jas de Bouffan

This residence is about a mile to the south-west of Aix; it was rebought after the death of Cézanne's mother and is still private property. Cézanne lived here for forty years.

The last residence of Cézanne

Cézanne died at 23 rue Boulegon, in 1906 at the age of 67. He lies in the Saint-Pierre cemetery.

Museums in Aix

The Granet museum, Saint-Jean-de-Malte square, tel. 04 42 38 14 70. Eight canvasses by Cézanne retrace the eight main stages in his work. But in the same museum one can also see fine paintings of Aix from the Belle Epoque, by Louise Germain, Louis Gauthier and Joseph Ravaisou.

Cézanne's studio, Atelier des Lauves, 9 avenue Paul Cézanne, tel. 04 42 21 06 53. Watercolours, original drawings and a few souvenirs are displayed here.

Aix-en-Provence, a charming town with calm squares. Above: Albertas Square.

Town Hall Square.

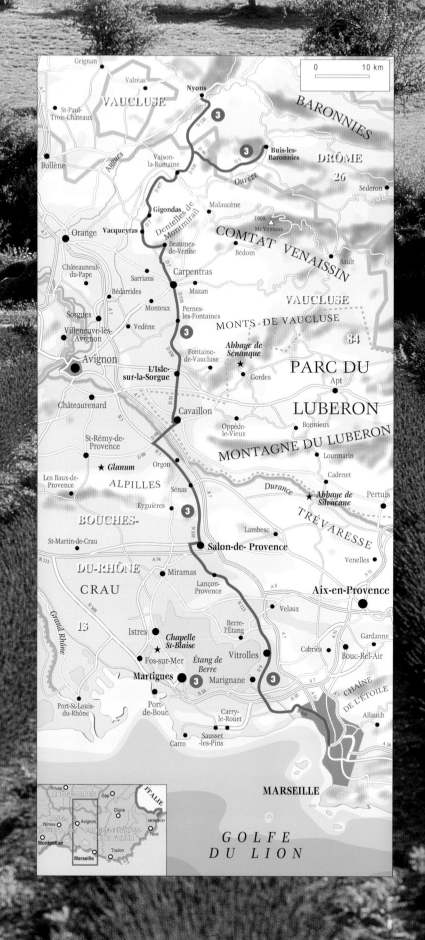

The savours route ...

... perfumes, colours, all good things from Provence

Buis-les-Baronnies: lime trees
Nyons: olive oil
Dentelles de Montmirail: Gigondas and Vacqueyras, wines of love
L'Isle sur-la-Sorgue: second-hand shops
Salon-de-Provence: soap
Aix: the calisson
Camargue: the poutargue
Marseilles: pastis

This is a path unlike anything else, winding its way between vineyards and fields of lavender. This truants' route does not include all the good things that the countryside dispenses without economising. It describes special preferences, and wishes, follow-ing a capricious and personal whim, the desire for a heady red wine on the tip of the tongue, rather than the penetrating gentleness of a *Baume-de-venise*. One can change direction at the last second, just as it happens on a journey when one pays attention to one's feelings and can arrive at the very edge of Fontaine-de-Vaucluse only to turn away, horrified by the overcrowding on the terrace and by the number of cars in the car-park.

A route like this is space, freedom... a jealous and intimate desire.

Buis-les-Baronnies: the name already makes one dream. One imag-

In the Baronnies landscapes, nature is beautiful, both gentle and wild.

Colette's springtime

Colette describes her vision of the Provençal countryside seen at dawn, from the famous "Blue Train" which carried her to the South: "Springtime arrived during my journey, springtime as one imagines it in fairy stories, exuberant, ephemeral, the irresistible Southern spring, solid, fresh, surging with sudden patches of greenery, with long grasses waving, mottled in the wind, with mauve Judas trees, with paulownia the colour of grey periwinkle, with laburnums, wisteria, roses..."

49

The Baronnies: the regard embraces long horizons...

ines a country with a long history, with an antique Mediterranean forest, with an air perfumed sublimely by lime blossoms, with vast silvery fields of olive trees interrupted by the capricious expanses of the garrigue. The Ubrieux gorges, the Saint-Julien rock mark the site in its niche sheltered from the winds, the Ouvèze bathes it, gently.

Buis is the chief town of the Baronnies canton, a territory which holds several very beautiful villages, such as Mollans-sur-Ouvèze, with its Dauphin fountain and its wash-house, Mérindol-les-Oliviers now in ruins, and the hamlets of the Plaisians, a beautiful terrace on Mont Ventoux.

The lime trees of the Baronnies have been known for ever, and especially appreciated. In existence since the beginning of the XIXth century, the

Market square at Buis, the chief town of the Baronnies.

50

Nyons, with its bridge which can be seen from afar.

present plant was obtained through selection, and the excellent quality of the stock gives flowers which are big and very perfumed; during harvesting which is between June and July the heady perfume invades the town. Every year, on the first Wednesday of July, the lime fair animates Buis. They celebrate this precious tree which offers the Baronnies 90% of the national production, nearly 450 tons a year, or about 10

Olive oil from Nyons is one of the most appreciated by the best palates.

kilos per tree!

The weighing takes place using antique Roman scales, the price is then fixed, business deals made between connoisseurs who feel and breathe in the perfume of the flowers. The harvesting takes place in five cantons: Buis-les-Baronnies, Nyons, La Motte-Chalancon, Rémuzat and Séderon.

Nyons is not very far from Buis. The landscape has already changed, and the Roman bridge is recognisable from afar. Nyons is proud of its olive oil, present in all the shop windows, in all its boutiques. In one way or another, everything in Nyons reminds one of this marvel: it is in fact an absolutely delicious oil, which both French and foreign gourmets appreciate as it deserves, classified AOC, of guaranteed origin.

What is a scourtin?

It is a filter for olive oil, antique, traditional, whose name comes from the Provençal escourtin which means a flat basket. It is circular in shape and can be found in the Roman oil mills, the only difference being that at that time the scourtins were made of straw or textiles, and now they are made of coconut fibre. This substance which makes up the husk of the nut, that is the outer envelope of the shell, has proved to be very resistant, and has been adopted after trying alfa-grass from the Sierras and the Atlas.

The technique of scourtins goes back to Antiquity: their origin dates from the Greeks and Romans.

51

Photo Eric Cattin

The earth, the sky, and the olive trees of the Baux-de-Provence.

The olive, a sacred and blessed tree was the first tree to emerge from the waters, according to the Old Testament, to tell Noah and his family that their punishment was over and that life could begin again on Earth.

In Rome, Minerva, Goddess of Wisdom, taught the art of cultivating the olive.

A sacred tree: in common belief as well as in the leading monotheistic religions, the unction symbolises the link between man and God. In the Catholic religion, sacred also, this oil obtained from the mythic tree whose branches decorate the churches on Palm Sunday. Holy oils have always been used for the ordination of priests, for baptisms and for the extreme unction.

The olive is harvested beginning in September. The green olives come first, while the black olives continue to mature during the whole of the month of October. The fruits intended for the mill are only picked in December. All depends on the climate and varies from one zone to another.

The ways of picking the olives vary as well, depending on the use and the purity of the oil one wishes to obtain. Certainly, picking by hand preserves the fruit best of all, since it has not been damaged by nets or falls, and does not become mouldy which would harm the degree of acidity of the oil later.

These days, to simplify things, the system of using a comb with long teeth passed through the leaves, is usually used.

To obtain one litre of olive oil, one needs eleven pounds of olives. A good picker can collect about 75 per day...

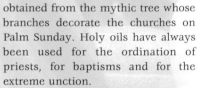

The oil mill of C. Rossi, at Mouriès, produces an oil with a precious savour.

Olive oil and health

Recent studies have proved that the Mediterranean diet helps decrease cardio-vascular problems. Olive oil in particular has positive effects on health. In the stomach, it does not alter the gastric acidity, but helps the liver and the gall bladder, encouraging easy and regular evacuation of the bile to the intestine, resting the liver and not changing the cholesterol content of the bile.
It helps digestion and protects arteries and veins thanks to its anti-oxidising high vitamin E content. It lowers blood viscosity, responsible for thromboses, and reduces the probability of arteriosclerosis.
This marvel even keeps the brain clear, protecting it from ageing and from toxic, immunological and viral aggressions.

Spain and Greece are the major producers of olive oil, but their harvesting system is usually mechanical. Their production is not as careful as in the Baronnies.

In Italy, in the Chianti, they have turned towards manual picking. As a result, the Tuscany oils like those of the Baronnies, treated as precious nectars, demand high prices and can be proud of their AOC name.

The pressing method to extract the oil goes back to more than six thousand years. Olive oil was always extracted by simple methods, which were still used in Syria in the XIXth century. The olives were pounded in a mortar, and the paste put into an earthenware jug, and next hot water was poured on top and the mixture masticated by hand. Since the oil was lighter than the water, it rose to the top. These days, after sorting, the olives are washed in cold water to eliminate impurities and then crushed without taking out the

stones, in the mill. The thick paste is matured and made unctuous by kneading. And then it is divided into about 12 pounds per scourtin (filter) piled one on top of the other. Finally, it is submitted to hydraulic pressure to extract the juice of the olive. This is called cold first pressing virgin olive oil. The oil extracted is then decanted by centrifuge. Its appearance, its taste and its acidity are checked. Second quality oils are then sent to the refineries to end up in soap works.

La "Tanche"

In Nyons, La Tanche is the fruit of a long passion between the town and the olive tree, between the peasant and his land. The name of "Tanche" given to olive oil is the proof. Here, it is called by its real name...

The method of pressing to extract the oil goes back six thousand years.

Dentelles de Montmirail

The needle-points of Montmirail scratch the chin of the sky.

Wines of the apocalypse, velvet and coal: the gigondas which caresses the throat - (left) - and the vacqueyras which scratches it.

Gigondas, Vacqueyras and their "terroir"

Gigondas and Vacqueyras are two of the most formidable guaranteed origin wines in the Rhône valley.

When one sees the Dentelles de Montmirail from far away, stone fingers scratching the sky, one becomes slightly thirsty. This is because here the wines have the character of the land (terroir).

On this dry soil, almost inhospitable, the vines grow prodigiously and the grape becomes drunk from the brutal sun on the slopes. The vines are cut right down, so that their juice is concentrated, and their roots pierce the mineral soil, which is not easy.

These mountains were formed by the imperceptibly slow but violent collision of two huge land blocks. Layers and layers were overturned by this collision between sand and silt, deposited by ancient rivers, on other fossil beds. The Dentelles were born from this apocalypse.

What differentiates one wine from another? The answer lies in the soil, the topography, the climate, the vine itself of course, and the hand of man.

The soil, the topography (slope and altitude) and climate together constitute the "terroir", a very French word which is now understood throughout the world.

Grenache, Syrah and Mourvedre grapes which are the components of Gigondas and Vacqueyras, are perfectly adapted to this soil and this climate.

The Gigondas and Vacqueyras appellations are very recent: 1971 for the first and 1990 for the second.

In the glass, wonderful spicy fruits, golden red... apart from the price. One of the latest infatuations of wine connoisseurs.

Second-hand at L'Isle-sur-la-Sorgue

Second-hand dealing!

Furniture and objects from the regional heritage are found side by side in the boutiques of L'Isle-sur-la-Sorgue, one of the favourite meeting points of second-hand dealers, antiques enthusiasts or simply the curious. At L'Isle, one can find beautiful straw-bottomed or tapestry upholstered chairs, magnificent benches in golden straw, painted cupboards, lots of so-called "Louis XV style" furniture, quilted bed-covers as well as old textiles, "quick fired" faience from Moustiers with its bright colours, and delicate faience decorated with little flowers, which is likely to come from Marseilles. But, one has to know, nothing that is really beautiful is cheap. It is up to you to play the game.

At L'Isle-sur-la-Sorgue, one can spend hours watching the transparent water flowing over a bed of pebbles... preferably with a pastis in one's hand...

At Sault, even out of season, the air still smells of lavender.

Perfumed rolls stretching to infinity, mauve colours on a Sienna earth.

Lavender is omnipresent along the roads of the countryside. It rolls out in long sinuous lines from Sault to Valréas, from Gordes to Banon, winds round Mont Ventoux, and lies under the magnificent village of Simiane-la-Rotonde. Finally, even though it is sovereign nearly everywhere, it is between Séderon, Banon and Sault that most is produced; 70% of French production. To obtain 1 kilo of essence, one has to distil 125 kilos of fine lavender, for 42 kilos of lavandin, hybrid lavender.

At present the price of a kilo of pure essence is between 350 and 400 FF, while that of lavandin essence is 60 FF.

The difference between the two plants is evident, apart from the price and the appearance: bigger and cultivated in the plains, lavendin is a hybrid species which comes from crossing fine lavender with spike, a common species, reproduced by grafting and whose camphered essence is the raw material in many household goods, cleaning products, soap powders and soaps.

As for the precious fine lavender, real or official, it is cultivated at an altitude between 1970 and 4920 feet, and flowers in July. It is given a guaranteed origin appellation, and its essence is used in "noble" preparations, medicinal and cosmetic.

A little tip: a drop of essential oil of lavender is perfect for healing a pimple very quickly.

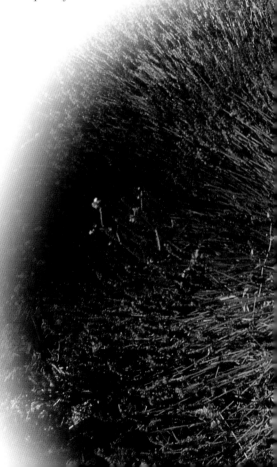

Photo Eric Cattin

Photo Eric Cattin

The history of lavender

Lavender, whose name comes from the Latin lavare, meaning to wash, has been known from Antiquity.

This rock-loving plant came from Persia and the Canaries, and was introduced into France by the Phocaeans at the same time as the vine and the olive tree. It acclimatised so well in this country of dry hills that it became habitual, bending in the wind of the Mistral, mixing with the wild rosemary whose flowers hardly make any impression on the waving mauve, running from plain to sunny knolls.

The Ancients had discovered its medicinal and antiseptic virtues, and lavender was used in several medicines, the best known being the Thériaque composition, an antidote to animal venom. Its calming, insecticide, anti-rheumatism and sedative properties were widely used, like a sort of all-inclusive elixir. As for the Romans, more hedonist, who appreciated its aromatic qualities, they perfumed their baths and their clothes with lavender.

In the Middle Ages, medical tracts also mentioned lavender for its disinfectant powers. It was scattered on the floors of dwellings, and its essence was burned in houses infested with the plague to try to stop the spread of the epidemic.

In the XVIIIth century, Madame de Sévigné recommended rubbing oneself twice a day with an ointment with a base of lavender and bitter almonds, to keep away the fleas. The marquise also sniffed "the Queen of Hungary's water" composed of lavender, rosemary and marjoram: "It is divine", she wrote. "I become drunk with it every day, I keep it in my pocket. It is a folly like tobacco; when one is used to it one cannot do without it."

At the same time, at the Court, perfumes were the rage. Everything had to be pleasantly perfumed; gloves, handkerchiefs, wigs... It was also one way to mask the sometimes obtrusive odours in the châteaux, since their bathrooms were not perfect.

In the XIXth century, enthusiasm for perfumes reached all the social classes. Consumption of lavender essence rose dramatically; prices soared, and lavender harvesting increased.

But one had to wait for the 1920's to see the first great plantations of lavender appear; the "lavanderaies". Since then, for our great pleasure, Provence perfumes the cupboards of discreet young girls, an odour of cleanliness and sleep in white sheets dried in the sun.

Black diamond

The truffle (truffe) is known under different names: tuber melanosporum, black diamond... but in Provence it is called the "rabasse".

It is also called the Périgord truffle, but often it has only the name from this region, since the truffle prefers the départements of the South East. The truffle is the source of great envy and many secrets. This underground mushroom can be extracted by digging at the feet of oak trees, white and green, and hazel-nut trees. Different methods of excavation are used: flies, pigs, or dogs - dachshunds and terriers are said to be the best. Truffles ripen from the end of November to the end of March, and are excellent between January 15th and February 15th.

All this makes me hungry... I'd love a slightly runny omelette with slivers of truffle.

Soap by dates

At the beginning of the XVIIIth century there were about fifteen soap-works which made Marseilles the leading centre of the Mediterranean for producing and exporting soaps based on olive oil and natural sodas. This was the beginning of the prosperous era with a law in 1688 concerning the manufacture and marking of soap.

1760 : 28 factories, with 126 boilers, produced 9,000 tons of soap.

1823 : new oils arrived (palm, coco) and the first exact theory of saponification was published by Chevreuil.

1863 : a growth crisis. Nonetheless, demand continued to rise. Before the XXth century, the role of soap in domestic hygiene became predominant.

1906 : 142,777 tons were produced by the Marseilles soap-works and advertising as well as packaging made their appearance.

1913 : world conflict, certain factories disappeared and production dropped to 53,000 tons in

1918. When the Second World War broke out, the Marseilles soap industry had not recovered the level of production it had before the great depression. The soap industry collapsed, since artificial detergents from America had appeared and, in addition, washing machines began to be bought by households. Marseilles soap lost its role as a product of first necessity: it was difficult to fight against the Parisian perfumers who invaded the bathrooms. Four industries resisted this stagnation, at Salon-de-Provence and at Marseilles. But over the past fifteen years, the desire for natural products and the development of ecological ideas has brought soap from Marseilles back into fashion.

Present-day worker in an old setting; the Soap ecomuseum of Volx.

Soap, its qualities, nothing but qualities...

It is natural, thanks to the raw materials used in its production.

It is gentle, does not aggress the skin, and is recommended for washing clothes in contact with the skin.

It is efficient, dermatologists are not mean with their praises for its disinfectant action and its quasi-medicinal properties.

It is environmentally friendly, its biodegradability is rapid and almost total in the aquatic medium. In addition, it requires very little plastic wrapping.

It is economical, and its cost ridiculously low compared to all other hygienic products.

Twenty-four French factories now produce soap "from Marseilles". Here are a few addresses :

Photo Eric Cattin

* Compagnie du savon de Marseille, CSM-66, Chemin de Sainte-Marthe, 13014 Marseille.

* La Savonnerie Le Serail, 50 boulevard Anatole-de-la-Forge, 13014 Marseille. Enterprise founded in 1949 by Vincent Boetto.

* La Savonnerie Rampal-Patou, 71 rue Félix-Pyat, 13300 Salon-de-Provence.

* La Savonnerie Marius Fabre, 148 avenue de Grans, 13300 Salon-de-Provence: one of the oldest southern soap factories, founded in 1900 by Marius Fabre. A marvel which can be visited, and excellent products.

One should also note the Soap Ecomuseum near Manosque. It was founded by the Occitan society which presents the know-how of the master soap-makers and the evolution of manufacturing techniques, under the form of a permanent exhibition.

Donation l'Occitane - Les Fours-à-Chaux - 04130 Vol.

With the coming of the *"advertising"* era, soap found the words to attract its customers.

The calisson d'Aix

Mixing almonds and candied fruits is an old gastronomic idea which is not exclusive to the south of France : the Mediterranean countries adopted it one by one at some moment in their history.

The associated sweatmeats were called calisone in Italy – now the name is a Ricciarello – and kalistsounia in Greece. In Aix, it made its appearance in 1473, at the wedding reception of King René. The almond shape of the calisson is the subject of many legends, a mirror of the mandorla of the Cistercian abbeys, or the shape adopted by the queen's cook in loving homage.

In a magnificent old soap works, Marius Fabre, one can watch the saponification process... and buy some soaps.

Nostradamus, predictions up until 3797!

At Salon-de-Provence, there is a museum which cannot be missed: it holds the collections of manuscripts of Nostradamus and was his home from 1547 until his death. This Magus who peered into the future until 3797 wrote his Prophecies here. He studied medicine, pharmacy, astrology, humanism and was in contact with Rabelais, Catherine de Médici, Marguerite de Navarre and other great names of this world. The museum also displays objects from the XVIth century: plague tongs, pharmacy pots, scientific objects...

From this fresco, Nostradamus dominates a street in Salon-de-Provence, the town where he died.

Photo Eric C.

The poutargue

This a very particular speciality, as highly appreciated as caviar by connoisseurs, and is a preparation based on mullet roe. At the time of reproduction, in September, the mullets swim back up the estuary of the Petit Rhône and the Rhône. The fishing takes place in **Camargue** and at **Martigues**, using big nets called *calens*, operated by a swivel. The eggs are recuperated, extracting them delicately in two bunches, without tearing the very fine membrane protecting them. These eggs, extracted when they are mature, must be pink and of a coded size. Then, for several hours, they are placed on a dish, covered with fine salt and turned regularly so that they absorb the humidity.

Flattened, the two pockets are reduced to a maximum thickness of about 5 millimetres, using a spatula and a weight. They are then dried or smoked, and become very hard.

The poutargue is eaten grated on toast with olive oil, in spaghetti sauce or in very fine slices. One can also mix it with butter to add to grilled fish at the moment of serving. The sales price of poutargue can easily reach 1,000 FF the kilo. It can be found at Saintes-Maries, in the fish-shops of Martigues, and of course in very good groceries.

The telline

This is a little shellfish about one inch long and elongated in shape. It is also known under the name of sea bean.

It is a culinary speciality of **Saintes-Maries**, but can easily be found on all the markets of Provence, where it simmers in big cauldrons which smell of garlic and herbs.

Perfect for a bite at the end of the morning, with a – first? – glass of rosé. It will be served in a greaseproof paper cone, and you nibble it with your fingers.

Pastis

Among the different plants which grow in Provence, there is one which, like lavender, has become the symbol of the little daily pleasure of life in Provence: anise.

It is mentioned in the writings of the Babylonian empire, which makes one think that this plant was already used in a variety of medicinal preparations. The Chinese considered anise as a plant full of virtues and used it in the composition of various potions. Another plant, the absinth, was considered to be able to cure stomach problems.

In France, in 1263, the anise growers formed a brotherhood and practically monopolised its use for preparing ointments, elixirs, liqueurs, oils etc.

The evolution of this brotherhood is not well known, but nearly seven centuries later another organisation was created, "l'Ordre International des Anysetiers". The different pastis come from a mixture of alcohol concentrated at 96.3% , anise essence, star anise from the distillation of Chinese anise, liquorice powder, water, sugar and infusions whose proportions are kept secret. This preparation is macerated for two to three

Photo Eric Cattin

weeks. It is then filtered and checked before bottling, and there are various brands on sale in the markets, in the groceries and the cafes...

These days, there are still several big names. The most known are Ricard, Pernod (united in the same group since 1974), Casanis, Duval, Janot, Berger.

The "pastaga" is still the most appreciated aperitif in France : 2.5 milliard glasses for the summer season alone.

Three ways of drinking pastis in Provence

Le Perroquet : 1 dose of Pastis, 1 dose of mint syrup and 5 doses of water.

La Mauresque : 1 dose of Pastis, 1 dose of orgeat syrup, 5 doses of water.

La Tomate : 1 dose of Pastis, 1 dose of grenadine syrup, 5 doses of water.

This is to be poured with precaution - and moderation - into a glass dimmed with a million fine droplets, while the ice cubes tinkle in the cloudy water...

61

*Very Provençal
Indian fabrics.*

Right page:
**On the markets of Provence,
the nose, the mouth and the
eyes are subject to a severe test.**
Berlingots photo: Eric Cattin.

Provençal textiles...

... are Indian! The coloured textiles which Provence is so proud of come, originally, from India. The first Indian cottons arrived in **Marseilles** in the XVIIth century, and the inhabitants of Provence, who until then had only known embroidered or woven textiles, discovered the "Indians". The master card-makers, manufacturers of playing cards who knew how to make wood engravings, started manufacturing these textiles directly in Marseilles and Avignon, which had been imported until then. The colours were taken from Provençal plants; the yellow of the gorse, the red of the madderwort... Marseilles, a free port, and the comtat Venaissin, territory of the Pope, could continue producing Indian fabrics after the prohibition of the King under the pressure of the French textile industry... it came too late, since at the Court of Versailles there was a compromise about selling and buying the forbidden Indian fabrics. The Versailles nobles protected their suppliers. Trade became free only in 1759.

The pretty villages route

Lourmarin
Bonnieux
Lacoste
Ménerbes
Oppède
Goult
Gordes
Roussillon
Saint-Saturnin-les-Apt
Rustrel
Saignon
Sivergues
Buoux

The strange destiny of this micro-region, so prettily designed between hills and valleys, so magnificently scattered with remarkable architecture and sumptuous natural sites... a weird destiny, multiple, as well as posh, but if you search attentively in its innermost recesses, you will find the authentic.

Authentic, when in the summer they talk with a snobbish Parisian accent in the markets?

Authentic, when from above one is blinded by the endless turquoise swimming pools set in the *mas* which have been restored down to the last stone?

Authentic, when Peter Mayle, former English advertiser converted to writer, denounces in his books, with love and humour but also with bitterness, the false-real inhabitants, the covetous and backward enterprises, the inflated products which follow the fashion, the prices, close to those of rue du Bac in Paris?

Peter Mayle, victim of his own success, has left for regions more clement for his pen; several stylists and other journalists have given up, since these villages have become impossible in summer. They have gone to the wider spaces of Tuscany where the almost untouched expanses – they think – remain to be conquered.

The Luberon (pronounced "Lubeu-ron" and not "Lubéron") and the neighbouring villages are feasible in spring and autumn. It is true that in summer one comes across boiling tourist buses on the sun-drenched roads,

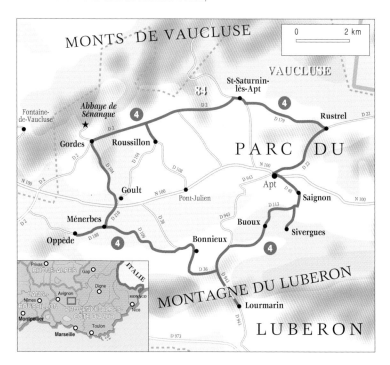

Pronounce it "Lubeuron"!

The villages of the Luberon appeared in the Middle Ages, hooked onto the flanks of the rocks, around water sources. They were built tall, next to a castle or a church, so close to the rocks that often the mineral element participated intimately in the arrangement of the rooms. The inhabitants of this region lived off the cultivation of olive trees and lavender, rearing sheep and from silk worms.
Traces of these ancient cultivations can still be seen in the little walls and enclosures of dry stones, and in the "bories", small stone cabins in which the peasants sometimes sheltered for weeks, during the time they were working in the fields.

The oldest part of the Lourmarin castle - above - dates from the xv[th] century.

but... but the season is short and here, in winter, it is cold. Good, we can close... and then the country itself opens up...

Here is a loop route, where one can potter, with several suggestions about how to discover these delicious villages.

Lourmarin

Lourmarin is at the foot of the Luberon, winding up in narrow and sinuous streets, around the rocky "Castellas", the belfry (the present clock) built on the site of the former medieval castle.

Lourmarin was an important merchant site from the xi[th] century. After that, looting and the plague chased out the inhabitants in the xiv[th] century. Around 1470, the Seigneur, Fouquet d'Agoult, installed families from the Vaudoise in the deserted village, in order to bring in people and exploit the land.

The very beautiful fountains of Lourmarain are worth stopping for, in the silence of the siesta hour for example, on the square freshened by their gentle drip-drip.

You have to see the " salt box " – the belfry – the Renaissance houses and, near the village, the country farms (bastides) from the xvi[th] and xviii[th] centuries, the Renaissance château in two parts, the older part dating from the xv[th] century. Every year the château receives pensioners, laureates from the Foundation for the Aix-en-Provence Academy.

Albert Camus, author of *L'Etranger*, lies in the village cemetery where he bought a house. In January 1960 the writer died in a car accident, at the entry to the village, on the Combe road from Bonnieux to Lourmarin.

Bonnieux

This village, perched on the northern slope of the Luberon, was Celtic-Ligurian by origin. It is dominated by its church, half-Romanesque from the xii[th] century and half-Gothic. In the Middle Ages it was the fief of the Counts of Forcalquier and Toulouse. Later is became pontifical land and summer residence for the Papal Court of Avignon, and remained an enclave of the comtat Venaissin until 1791.

In the i[st] century, the vast territory of Bonnieux was crossed by the Domitian Way (Cadiz-Milan).

At the Julian bridge (3 B.C.) 3 miles away, a Roman bridge celebrating its two thousand years, there was the junction with another ancient Way leading to Aix across the coomb. From here there is a magnificent view over the Vaucluse mountains and Mont Ventoux. Above the medieval village, with its old narrow streets, full of charm, the route of the Luberon Ridges begins, which crosses the "Forest of Cedars" a promenade bordered by immense hundred-year-old cedars. One reaches the new church (1870) by climbing up 86 steps in the shade of these cedars.

At Bonnieux there remain several examples of its flourishing past: traces of towers and the ramparts from the XIIIth century, the Rouville house from the XVIIIth which is now the town hall, and the Philippe tower which dates from the end of the XIXth century.

There is a Provençal market on Friday mornings.

Bonnieux deserves to be visited on foot. Its narrow alleys are full of "art de vivre" treasures...

Details from an old door. Angels and coats of arms.

*In the village of Lacoste,
which dominates the château
of the famous Marquis,
life is peaceful, and the hours
pass like honey
over a buttered sandwich.*

*In the deserted
narrow streets of Lacoste,
one's steps echo.*

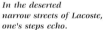

Lacoste

The village of Lacoste is known especially for the ruins of the château de Sade, but one risks being disappointed since the famous Marquis has not left any trace here. On the other hand, Lacoste is a tiny village where it is good to stay a while, with very beautiful houses which offer chambres d'hôte and its adorable cafe, nestled in the greenery. Lacoste is mentioned several times in *A Year in Provence*, for its prettiness and its good food. A small church from the XIIth century and the ramparts are all that is left from the past; at present the view and its "dolce vita" are the charms most looked for.

Ménerbes

Nostradamus had written in his notes that the village of Ménerbes extends on an elongated spur, in the shape of a ship, with its prow and its poop. It was already inhabited in the Palaeolithic era – Soubeyras shelter – and the Chalcolithic, the epoch of the Pichouno dolmen.

Traces of Roman villas have also been found, as well as the cave of the hermit Castor, who founded his monastery of Mananca. In the Middle Ages, access to the city, full of under-ground passages, was through the two gates of Saint-Sauveur and Notre-Dame, which figure in the form of two golden keys on the Ménerbes coat of arms. During the Wars of Religion, in the XVIth century, Ménerbes was submitted to a siege of fifteen months by the Catholic troops of the Pope and the King of France. The besieged finally left the town, but with full battle honours, all their banners flying. Even today the iron cannon-balls which rained down on Ménerbes during this historic siege are still preserved...

From the old cemetery, to the west, there is a magnificent panoramic view over the Luberon and the Vaucluse mountains.

Old Ménerbes jealously guards the sumptuous private houses of its past and present "happy few" owners. Thus, neither le Castellet, where the painter Nicolas de Staël lived, nor la Carmejane, l'hôtel de Tingry (XVIth century) nor the residence of the General of the Empire Robert, which became the property of Picasso, can be visited...

So what can one do? Well, for tireless tourists there is the Tire-Bouchon (Corkscrew) museum in the Citadelle domain, at the foot of the village.

Oppède

When one goes to Oppède, one is inevitably taken by the old village. In this medieval buttressed fortress, the houses of the villagers settled over the centuries between the castle and the ramparts. The old village was abandoned at the beginning of the XXth century, and only the lower part and several houses clinging to the rocky flanks are inhabited. These medieval and Renaissance houses, the church of Notre-Dame-Dalidon from the XVIth century, built on Romanesque infrastructures and restored in the XIXth century, this medieval castle in ruins, the chapels of the Pénitents from the XIIth century, Saint-Laurent and Saint-Antonin, exude a strange charm. Even the inhabited houses seem deserted... The stony path which leads to the top of the village, and to the castle, is usually empty. Only the romances of the birds, the monotonous song of the cicadas and the litany of the crickets accompany the walker. Behind the solid wooden doors, old stones and, perhaps, a fountain, a garden... Oppède is really one of the most intriguing sites of the Luberon: why is it not frequented any more? Why, when holiday houses flourish everywhere else, is it not the same thing here? A little cafe which also offers chambres d'hôte, at the entrance to Oppède-le-Vieux, has a few old cane chairs and a few unmatched tables under an arbour; the time for a glass of rosé, the time for a dream, one can imagine the calm and charm of a little house in the old village...

View from the ruined castle over the roofs of Oppède-le-Vieux.

In the recently restored church in Oppède, several rare visitors in the flickering light of a candle making a wish.

The Renaissance château of Gordes and the village, built with the stone of its foundation.

An old factory rehabilitated

The OKHRA Association and the commune of Roussillon, in collaboration with many partners, decided in 1988 to acquire the Mathieu factory, created in 1920.
The domain comprises 12 acres with two main buildings: that for yellow ochres, extracted, and that for red ochres, roasted.
The whole production chain was reconstituted by the factory with the aim of making it useful again: it is not a museum but a centre of activity.
Because of its role as a conservatoire, the factory endeavours to be didactic. Its aim is also to promote the ore and all the professions connected with it

Goult

A pretty village slightly hidden, restored with care and passion, with fine stone buildings in the ochre colours of the past, with arched passageways. Traces of old ramparts, the castrum dominating, with its posterns and its drawbridge, the château of the Agoult family which unfortunately cannot be visited, the Saint-Sébastien church, pure Romanesque, with its pointed barrel vaulting supported by arches, which shelters a baroque reredos, shady squares of centuries' old lotus trees make Goult a charming visit. It is also the gateway to a country of market gardening, fruit trees, vines and lavender.

The big olive groves, the fine evergreen oaks and the agricultural plantations surrounded by dry stone walling are looked after, restored and organised by volunteers from the Conservatoire des Terrasses.

Gordes

This is a village proud of its beauty, listed among the "most beautiful villages of France", on the edge of the Vaucluse plateau facing the Luberon. Gordes was built with the stone from the rock which serves as its base.

The Renaissance château dominates the village. It was rebuilt by Bertrand de Simiane on the foundations of the former fortress from the XIIth century, and for twenty years sheltered the Vasarely foundation, closed in 1996. The narrow paved streets with gutters on either side, the vaulted passages, the arcades and the steps in the old village have kept all their charm... To be avoided, however, during the tourist invasions.

Very close to Gordes is the village of the Bories, arranged around the bread oven, with its sheep-folds, its wine barrels, the spaces where they threshed the corn, the enclosures and the surrounding walls, evidence of the laborious work of innumerable generations. Their origin remains mysterious, even though one knows that the oldest date back to the Bronze Age and that the most recent were built in the XVIIIth century. This hamlet, listed as a "Historic Monument", is the biggest group of these dry stone dwellings typical of the country of Apt.

Roussillon shelters the rose colours of the twilight, hides them inside, and reflects them when evening comes.

In the park of the Stained Glass Museum one can also see the Moulin de Bouillons. This is the oldest olive oil mill conserved intact with all its working elements, including the press, made of a whole oak tree weighing 7 tons.

Not far from the mill is the village of Saint-Pantaléon which possesses a little Romanesque church with three naves, a site of strange beauty, somewhat morbid; the delightful church is surrounded by a rupestral necropolis with small tombs of children. As is so often the case in these places which are a little lost, the key is kept at the nearest house, for the most curious visitors. In fact it is a "respite sanctuary"; it was thought that children who died before being christened came back to life for the time of a mass, during which they were given the sacrament. Then, dying again, they were buried there.

The market is held in the village square on Tuesday mornings.

Roussillon

Light, mineral ardour, burnt earth against the blue of a sky metalled by so much fire: at the heart of the deposits, Roussillon is a village which, like the other stopping places on this route,

pleases because of its small squares and narrow alleys but which is, in addition, also made sublime through its colours. Unfortunately, what is true for Gordes, Ménerbes and Bonnieux is even more true for Roussillon: one risks looking at it badly and may not like it if one does not see it when it is calm. This is the great paradox of tourism, the irony of the end of the century: one wears out the beauty by too much admiration... The ochres of the façades, the trompe-l'œil of a window, a rose-coloured balcony flowered with the delicate blue of the plumbago, so many subtle emotions which need to be treated with solitary tenderness, taking one's time.

An extraordinary sight, the Giants' Way, at Roussillon.

Photo Eric Cattin

Why ochre?

Although used in decoration and by craftsmen for stucco, trompe-l'œil, painting on furniture, pottery and tinting, ochre is nonetheless used mainly in the building industry.

In Provençal tradition, plaster plays an important role in covering buildings: it constitutes the "envelope" of Provençal houses, giving them this light and this gentle apricot colour.

Mixed with granulates (sand) and bonding agents (cement, chalk), it ensures that the walls are sealed but can still breathe.

However, its greatest quality lies in its resistance to the heat and the light, which explains its use in all Southern countries.

The imposing mass of the church of Saint-Saturnin d'Apt, and the pretty houses of the old agricultural town.

The impressive Rustrel Colorado.

Saint-Saturnin-les-Apt

Saint-Saturnin-les-Apt is a village leaning against a rock upon which two windmills from the XVIIth century and the remains of a medieval castle stand guard.

Despite the recent villas which surround this agricultural town, Saint-Saturnin is a village full of history which deserves a certain attention. Some very beautiful old dwellings with sculpted porches still remain, with finely worked doors and window frames. In the ramparts district, one must not miss the Ayguier portal, then the vestiges of the castle, the XIth century chapel, the mills, the doors and towers from the XVth century.

The landscapes around Saturnin are delightful.

Rustrel

In the russet furrow of Roussillin, Rustrel is a tiny village tucked away at the foot of the Albion plateau in the Regional Nature Park of the Lube ron. The exploitation of ochre at the

Quarries which look like canyons

Over several miles, cliffs of gold and fire worthy of Colorado; quarries which look like canyons. Layers separated in isolated massifs at Roussillon, and in continuous bands between Rustrel and Gignac, sometimes reaching a thickness of 45 feet. This is the ochre which is responsible for all these marvels, one of the natural riches of Provence.

beginning of the century, meant that Rustrel became an important production centre and took part in the industrial revolution because of its ferruginous ores. Today, although the exploitation of the site is declining, this "Provençal Colorado" is beginning a new life by opening up to visitors, dazzled by the palette of colours of its cliffs.

Saignon

This village with its thousand inhabitants, perched high up, near the Claparèdes plateau, dominates the whole of the Calavon valley.

Saignon has been inhabited from Antiquity, proved by the existence of the vestiges of a group of houses dating from before the Roman Conquest. But Saignon was above all the key for defending Apt, a fortress with only a few archaeological traces remaining, like the three castles, the ramparts and the rampart walk.

After crossing the old village through steep alleys, fountain squares, and the fantastic natural fortress dug out by the winds, pierced with steps and secret passages, one comes across a superb panorama over the plains and the mountains. In good weather, one can see Mont Ventoux, the Lure mountain, the Alps of Upper Provence and the Luberon.

The XIIth century church, dedicated to Notre-Dame-de-Pitié, is a remarkable Romanesque building because of its dimensions and its pyramid-shaped bell tower. It has a nave with three bays which are prolonged into lateral chapels, and an apse covered with flat stones. The façade in tri-lobed arcades on pilasters is later than the edifice, as is the sculpted portal in solid wood from the XIVth century. One should also see the belfry, with its clock and an unusually simple bulbiform campanile, and the wash-house with three successive pools under a vault which has a staircase leading to the library.

The bishop's palace became a presbytery and then a private house: it is framed with remarkable dressed stones.

About one mile away, there is the Saint-Eusèbe abbey, founded in the XIIth century after the creation of a religious community installed by Saint Martian, born in Saignon in the VIIIth century, a hermit who lived in a cave.

Walking around the streets of the village, one can admire the squares and fountains – water is not lacking in Saignon– as well as several old houses with remarkable doors. There is also the Sainte-Marie church from the XIIth century, the ruins of the castle and of course the Saignon rock from which there is a splendid view over Apt and its surroundings.

Sivergues

In the village, a church dating from the end of the XVIth century, several fine buildings from the same epoch, the Castellas with the ruins of the Saint-Trophime church of the XIIth century, and the Vaudois cemetery. Rupestral tombs at the Crosses and the domain of Paris.

High up in the village there is a sheep farm, the Sardinian, which has been in existence for many years. It receives hikers for a night, and visitors for a meal around the family table. An address lost in nature, quite astonishing.

Buoux

The village at the bottom of the valley, with the superb Saint-Symphorien campanile - unfortunately private property – is tiny: there are several pretty farms lost amongst the fields of lavender, guest houses, a wash-house, a welcoming auberge, and the point of departure for the cliffs, for all mountain climbers. But Buoux has roots which go very far back: traces of ancient human installations have been found here, Neanderthal man who lived here for about 90,000 years. Later, after the last Würm glaciation, the caves were occupied up until the Neolithic period, about 6,000 years before Christ, first as dwellings and then as burial sites. The Buoux fort was built during the XIth century; one can visit these rather frightening ruins, which overlook a precipice of 250 feet...

Thus life at Buoux began under the

At Buoux, the Saint-Symphorien priory is private property. But those who look carefully can see its belfry from afar...

The Buoux cliffs

Since the first ways were opened with forged pitons up until the most difficult passages, the Buoux cliffs have told tales of a love of climbing which has lasted for many years. Buoux is a magic place, a little abrupt corner of Paradise where the Aiguebrun flows all year round.

At the highest point of the Fort rock there is a mystery which has not yet been solved. One can see, cut into the rock itself, a circular cup and a channel which extends for several metres.

Was it a system for pouring boiling oil onto a possible enemy; an ensemble of protohistoric sacrifice, or a medieval fire signal.

The cliff is made out of sedimentary rock, born of the succes-

sive piling of marine deposits: when climbing up three feet of rock, one covers twenty millennia of history on earth. The Buoux rock is unique and in great demand: without cracks, it has resisted frost and therefore time. Its name, from the Latin mola, or mill, comes from the fact that it was used for grinding millstones. The shapes of the cliff are round and welcoming, almost sensual. In the very middle of the valley is the Aiguille rock, in sandstone, a soft and rounded rock. With time, it has remained vertical whereas the limestone, which is a hard and brittle rock, is found in the form of scree.

Buoux can offer many ways of climbing; foliates, slopes, grooves, cracks and walls, but the holes remain the most frequently attacked.

rocks 125,000 years ago... In the village, there is a parish church dating from the end of the XVIth century. In the cemetery there is a pretty Romanesque church, Sainte-Marie, from the XIIIth century, with a single nave.

One has to climb up to the fort to enjoy the complete and exceptional panorama of the cliffs. Here one can see vaulted galleries, the ramparts, the fortifications and the arrow slits. But there is no doubt that the most impressive is the staircase carved out of the rock with its access postern. During the Wars of Religion, the Calvinists turned the castle into a Protestant fortification until 1660, the date when Louis XIV ordered that it should be destroyed.

Birth of an earth:
ochre

230 million years ago, Provence was covered by the sea. As time went by, the limestone of the sediments was coated with grey clay. Little by little, the sea retreated and Provence was exposed to a tropical climate with diluvial rains which washed the green sands, transforming them, gradually, into ochre sands. The iron was oxidised and gave this mixture of clay and sand all the colours and nuances of colours.

Generally, the ochre sands contain 90% of sand for 10% ochre. In Vaucluse, it is between 60 and 70% of ochre for only 30 to 40% of sand!

In Antiquity, ochre was used for ritual purposes, before being used for decoration. In Egypt, bodies traced in stone were coloured with ochre. But it was in Rome that they noticed that, in contact with fire, yellow ochre became red.

Jean Etienne Astier, from Roussillon, rediscovered the real quality of ochre and its unchanging colour, at the end of the XVIIIth century.

These days, even if they are far from the 40,000 tons produced at the beginning of the century, it is still used by craftsmen and in the building industry.

Only the Vaucluse deposit is still exploited, and only the yellow ochres are sold, since the reds are not luminous enough.

The extraction principle consists of spraying water through pipes on the walls of the quarries or digging underground galleries; the pressure then detaches the blocks which, carried by the current, end up in a spiral mixer where they are crushed, then carried away in small channels made of Oppède stone.

The biggest and heaviest sand is deposited first in the gutter while the other particles, finer and lighter, are carried by the water which by now is only transporting top quality pure ochre towards the basins.

Finally, the ochre is crushed by a mill, pulverised and roasted. Thus one

obtains a range of nuances from six initial pigments: Sienna earth, yellow ochre and light and dark earth shades give a total of seventeen variations of yellow, from violet to red passing through all the browns.

Firing is the most accurate way of controlling the tint of the finished product and its nuances.

In practice this is very subtle, since it depends uniquely on the criteria of sensitivity of the "ocrier" (odour, aspect of the smoke...).

The process which created the astonishing Rustrel Colorado marvel began 230 million years ago. At that time, the sands were green...
Photo: Eric Cattin.

The **Mediterranean route**

Before emptying frankly into the Mediterranean, the Rhône loses itself in the meanders of the Camargue, a flat and mysterious land. The most vast humid zone in Europe is caught, like a prey, in the claws of the water which, in its turn loses its way... "Eth-nostalgia for the mosquito years" is a

way of life, here where over the years and the civilisations, man has created the means to protect himself from the favourite beast of the swamps. From Aigues-Mortes to Cassis, the landscape changes with the history of man and the nature. One of the best adapted ways of discovering this coast is still the Little Train of the Blue Coast. The Estaque-Miramas line dates back to the beginning of the century. Certain stations have not changed since: l'Estaque, Niolon, Redonne-Ensuès... one passes by the fishermen's huts, some of them from the same epoch... one passes between a modernity which makes one

Summer in the calanques, enterprising youngsters offer cold water melons, bottles of cool water and various other drinks.
Opposite, the En-Vau calanque.
Photo Eric Cattin.

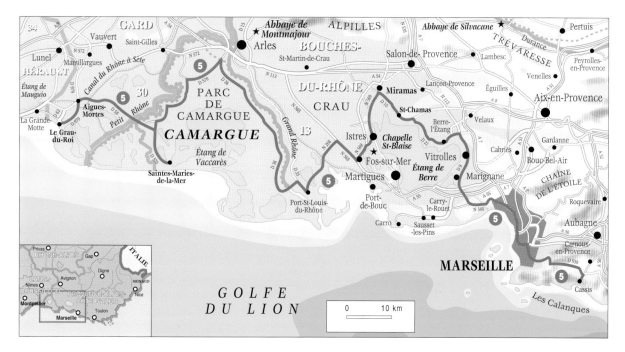

shiver sometimes, and the quivering of a time which was closer to the dreamt-of coast of this sea which was the cradle of our civilisation.

Aigues-Mortes,
Cité de Saint Louis

A melancholic town; suitable for the greyish colours, a town of bubbling "dead waters", majestic towers against the lunar salt pans, walls emerging from fairy-tale pools, reflecting in the marshy waters.

When Saint Louis started his first crusade, at the beginning of the XIIIth century, he was not rich: Montpellier belonged to the Counts of Toulouse, Marseilles to the Roman Empire; only the town of Aigues-Mortes was free as a base, as a port. This was not just by hazard, since the surrounding swamps were considered as very unhealthy. Despite this, Saint Louis created a port and, in 1246, drew up a franchise charter according all new residents Royal protection and

exemption from any taxes. The town was already built around the church; the ramparts were only built later, under the reign of Philippe le Hardi, son of Saint Louis.

Trade developed, helped by the Grau-Louis channel leading to the sea. There was even a lot of traffic, particularly pepper, spices, Genoa silk, ropes, nets, pottery, millstones from Spain, sugar and jams.

The first stage of the crusade, in 1248, started in Cyprus: the King of France and his wife Marguerite de Provence took to sea from the Grau channel.

This expedition was perfectly organised, and the manuscripts from the epoch give certain details: each member of the crew had a coffer which acted as trunk, bed, and in case of death, as coffin. Each had a barrel of fresh water, a lamp and a chamber pot. Despite this excellent organisation, the crusade went

Aigues-Mortes.

wrong after two years, and finished in Mansourah, where the King was taken prisoner.

In 1270, Saint Louis left Aigues-Mortes again, for Tunis. But the plague was there and he never returned from his second expedition.

In 1418, during the Hundred Years' War, the Bourguignons took Aigues-Mortes by surprise. They were then massacred, in their turn by the Armagnacs; they were thrown into a tower and covered with salt to avoid epidemics.

There is another famous tower in Aigues-Mortes, called "Constance". Constance was the sister of Louis VII, King of France. She married a Count from Toulouse, a hundred years before Aigues-Mortes was founded. To celebrate this alliance between Languedoc and the kingdom of France, the King's tower was given this name. Destined to protect the port, it was successively fortress,

Royal residence, lighthouse and State prison.

In the ramparts, built as a single entity 1815 yards round, there are only two entries to the north. But to the south, for the quays, five small doors were pierced: the Organeau, the Moulins door, the Galions, the Marine, and finally the Mèche door.

The melancholic beauty of Aigues-Mortes, the town of "Dead Waters", is partly due to its defensive architecture. Below, the Marine entrance. Above, a detail of the elegant stairs of one of the towers, which reminds one of the heart of an arum lily.

The salt marshes of the South

Since ancient times, salt has been collected in the region. The 400,000 tons of salt in stock form real white hills, looking like a Martian landscape. The salt workers, or saliniers, used to have a life expectancy of 25 years. The rosée du sel *is, for Salins a little like the* fleur de sel *for Guérande: at dawn, at the surface of the salt pans a slight crystallisation is formed, reserved in the old days for the owners of the salt marshes. Slightly humid and only slightly crunchy, this* rosée *is wonderful for raw preparations to be dipped in salt, but also on fine grilled foods and fish whose aromas are enhanced. A battle of flavours between Brittany and Provence, which is far from over...*

Photo Eric

Horse riding and life in contact with nature: the guardians. D.R.

Le Grau-du-Roi

To begin with, the Grau was only a group of fishermen's huts on the banks. It was only towards the middle of the XIXth century that the village separated from Aigues-Mortes. These days Le Grau-du-Roi is a traditional place where one can see the trawlers returning from Camargue.

The best promenade is without any doubt the walk beginning at the Espiguette lighthouse: wild nature, nothing but dunes and the sea, mile after mile, step after step...

The Camargue

The Camargue, wild and mysterious, a unique natural region, an amphibious territory whose ecological balance has miraculously been preserved over the years did not always look like it does today. The Rhône delta – a river whose bed has changed several times over the centuries – is an immense alluvial plain,

and the present Camargue, which covers hundreds of thousands of acres, is the result of the unceasing combat between the river, the sea, and man. It is dotted with lagoons, the biggest of which, the Vaccarès lagoon, is part of the Camargue Regional Park, created in 1972. The park also includes the Malagroy lagoon, the so-called "Imperial" lagoon, the Rièges woods, the whole covering about 200,000 acres.

The Camargue is flat: its altitude varies from 15 feet above sea level at its highest point to 5 feet below sea level at the bottom of the Vaccarès lake. Its limits are the two outlets of the Rhône (the Grand and the Petit Rhône), the city of Arles and the Mediterranean shore, in a territory between Montpellier, Avignon and Marseilles. The Camargue offers a diversity of natural environments where numerous fragile ecosystems interact. This exceptional biological wealth is produced by the contributions of water and salt. The population is small: less than 10,000 people live in Camargue divided into the communes of Saintes-Maries-de-la-Mer, Arles and Port-Saint-Louis-du-Rhône.

The Camargue, with its changing and unconquered aspect, opens up to visitors with its beaches, its marshes, its endless steppes and pastures, its original vegetation mixed with present cultivations.

The geomorphology of this vast territory was formed slowly under the dominant action of the Mistral, which blows in a north-westerly direction. The stretches of water are freshwater or salty, and give rise to flora characteristic of humid terrains, saltwort and low garrigue; near the dike to the sea, marram grass, couch grass, spurge and sand lilies bloom.

However, there are wooded spaces in Camargue which offer the

original Mediterranean mixture, a perfumed alliance of rosemary, daffodils, iris and lilacs, as in the Rièges wood. It is a paradise for birds, both for migrators and those which stay all year round. There are 323 different species, including evidently one of the emblems of the Camargue, the

Horses and bulls live in Camargue in complete liberty.

Photo Eric Cattin

The pink flamingo

This is the emblem of the Camargue – the only place in France where it nests and one of the very rare places in the Mediterranean. The population can reach about 20,000 couples, grouped into colonies. Its bright pink legs, disproportionately long, and fragile in appearance, carry a rather large body with pink tinges, brighter at the neck and the chest.

The underneath of the wings, carmine red which can only be seen when it is in flight, contrast with the deep black of the wing quills.

The neck, long and flexible, supports a head dressed with a humped beak, pink at the base and black at the tip, while the eye is bright yellow.

In order to fly, its tactics are to take several rapid strides in take-off, and then the legs and neck are stretched out – which creates a strange parallel ensemble. This is how the flamingo travels, this strange red, pink and black flying creature. Its powerful beak enables it to draw in water and then evacuate it through a layered filtering system, conserving only the plankton on which it lives. There are six species and sub-species of flamingo in the whole world

The Camargue horse

At the beginning, the horse was the real companion of the *manadier*, or livestock owner and the guardian, for sorting out the bulls and for agricultural work. Its solidity and hardiness come from its origins and the conditions of breeding; the horses live in the open all year round and develop strong resistance to climatic variations. The Camargue breed of horse was officially recognised in 1978, the date when the genealogical register was started, kept by the Regional Nature Park.

The foals are born with a dark brown coat, and become light grey when they reach adulthood, when they are about five years' old.

Above:
323 bird species live in Camargue, or transit the marshes. Above, the Vaccarès lake.

Opposite:
The Camargue horses are used to spending the winter in the open. This is a strong race, which was officially recognised very recently, in 1978.

pink flamingo. But there are also little egrets, grey night herons, bitterns, mallards, blue-headed wagtails, which are the usual guests of these special places. In the zone near the dike to the sea, one finds terns, avocets, Kentish plovers, gulls and seagulls.

In winter, up to 200,000 birds come here in the bad season.

The last beavers, foxes, various rodents and of course wild boar, have taken up residence in Camargue.

The Camargue bull

Its origins date back to earliest antiquity, since this bovine with its black or dark brown coat is considered to be the last "ramification" westwards of a race from Asia Minor. It lives in herds called *manades* (from the Provençal *manado* : a handful). Its breeding grounds are vast and, like the horse, its "all terrain" hardiness is the reason for its strength and its beauty in open-air breeding conditions. It is rarely more than four feet high for the males and the weight varies between 300 and 450 kilos.

The horned cattle of Camargue are bred essentially for taurine entertainments: cockade races, abrivado, bandi-

do, when they are not put to death, but also novilladas and corridas, which end with the death of the bull from this "brave" breed.

A little history, a little geography

Since ancient times, man has been dependent on the whims of elusive nature in this wild land: the Camargue with its herds of animals is regularly flooded.

The building of the dike to the sea, over twelve miles long, dates back to 1859 and allowed the salty waters to rise in the south of the territory.

Ten years later, the Rhône was provided with an embankment to limit the floods which until then had regularly covered the cultivated lands. These works made it possible to create rice fields, to plant cereals and form prairies in the north of the Camargue. The Camarguais practised irrigated viticulture and, after the Second World War, intensive rice-growing.

The following decades were devoted to building a system of irrigation and drainage canals to bring in fresh water from the Rhône.

To the south, extends the kingdom of salt and the Camargue of pink fla-

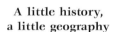

The bulls of the Camargue are the descendants of a race from Asia Minor.

83

An escapade

If you wish to discover this vast salty area, dominated by the sea winds and the marshes, horse-riding by the lagoons, the rice fields and the huge manades, *with a little taste of adventure, remains one of the most natural ways.*
It is also the best way to approach the guardians of the bulls, the pink flamingos and the wild ducks.
The best bicycle rides follow the "dike to the sea" which links the Salin de Giraud in the Arles commune to Saintes-Maries-de-la-Mer, taking the marked paths which lead to the bird sanctuary of Pont-de-Gau, a marvel which should be seen at sunrise. One can also follow the shore of the Vaccarèe lake, between the domain of Méjanes and the Cacharel mas.

Saintes-Maries-de-la-Mer
Right: Sara the patron
of the Gypsies.

mingos, black bulls and white horses, lakes and reed beds, lagoons of brackish water and salt steppes with sparse thickets of tamaris.

Beyond the dunes, a huge beach of fine sand extends over 30 miles of the Mediterranean coast.

Between the two domains, the Vaccarès lake, the pivot of the balance of the Camargue, regulates the levels of salinity of the water.

Above all, the Camargue is a land of oppositions where rigour and tolerance, fluctuations and balances, abundance and desert, paradox and reality, confront each other every day.

Around Vaccarès

The National Reserve

Created in 1927, it extends over about 30,000 acres, a territory stretching from the north of the Vaccarès lake down to the sea. It is a mixture of humid freshwater and brackish zones. Public access is limited to the area of the dike to the sea and the Capelière domain, the information centre of the National Society for the Protection of Nature, which manages the reserve.

Saintes-Maries-de-la-Mer

Situated at the western end of the delta, on a narrow stretch of sandy ground, always at the mercy of the impetuous waters of the Mediterranean, the village of Saintes-Maries-de-la-Mer – the biggest in

Camargue – is a well known sea resort. Its fortified church, built in the XIIth century on the site of a former Gallo-Roman sanctuary, shelters the relics of the blessed Maries : Marie Salomé, mother of the apostles James and John, and Marie Jacobé, sister of the Virgin, who came to the region as evangelists upon the death of Christ. The

*Miramas, a medieval village
north of the Berre lagoon,
must not be missed.*

statue of their Egyptian servant Sara, patron of the Gypsies, is also kept in the crypt, covered with an astonishing collection of dresses and cloaks.

Pilgrimages to Saintes-Maries-de-la-Mer

The cult around Saint Sara and then the two Maries – the 24th and 25th of May respectively – has developed into very colourful ceremonies. The statues of the saints are carried to the beach. The priest, in a boat, blesses the sea and the faithful carrying the cross and the relics. During the week of May 24th, nearly eight thousand Gypsies come to install their caravans in the town to offer their devotion to Sara, their patron saint.

Around the Berre Lagoon

Miramas-le-Vieux and Saint-Chamas are two villages which should not be missed, to the north of the Berre Lagoon.

Miramas is a medieval village, overlooking fields of olive trees on the top of a promontory, with a XIIth century chapel, a XVth century church, the ruins of a castle and, above all, adorable antiquated houses, with beautiful stones the colour of the setting sun, with pine trees next to them... finally, all this magnificence is not the shoddy goods of a village with too many visitors, but the representation of Mediterranean life as one loves it.

Saint-Chamas also holds many surprises: an ancient bridge, the Flavian bridge, whose pilasters are surmounted

85

*The Flavian bridge
at Saint-Chamas.*

The Calanques, from Marseilles to Cassis

A certain physical preparation is required before walking in the Calanques Massif, together with a good map, water, and the normal equipment of a hiker. One should note that it is not allowed to bivouac, but those who are discreet enough still do so at the end of the first walking day, at the Sugiton Calanque or a little further on, at the Pierres-Tombées (fallen stones) Calanque, reached by approaching the sea. Nonetheless, one must remember that the ecosystem of the Calanques is fragile: whatever one does, one has to respect it! The rules in place are those of common-sense, even though they may not mean economy of pleasure: swimsuits, for example are articles on the way out... Spring and autumn are the best times to cross the calanques. In summer, access is forbidden under prefectoral law, in order to limit the risks of fires. Often it is very hot, but there is also the risk of the *Mistral* which can be

by lions and eagles; it is built of yellow limestone and white stones from the quarries of Calissane. The houses at the top of the village date from the last century: one has to climb up there and then find the narrow path which leads to the Virgin's chapel, among the olive trees. From there, one looks over the roofs of Saint-Chamas, and the little fishing port... Later, one climbs down again to drink a pastis at the Marine bar...

The Cosquer grotto and its mysteries

The Cosquer grotto is situated in the Calanques, near Marseilles, at Cape Morgiou. It is accessible through a tunnel 375 feet long whose entrance is 120 feet down. 27,000 years ago, this cave was accessible on foot, until the sea level rose. It was listed as a historical monument in 1992 and is now closed not only because of its dangerous access which has already been fatal for several visitors, but also to preserve its heritage which is unique in the world. This underwater cave shelters several dozen paintings and engravings dating back to 27,000 and 19,000 years ago: a variety of land animals, horses and chamois, about fifty hands, dozens of geometrical signs as well as an exceptional engraving of a man killed.

The most frequent motif, hands with truncated fingers, is surrounded with a red or black halo blown with a blow-pipe. According to specialists, this is linked to hunting. Certain hands are cut with incisions, very probably long after, when the rites and representations had evolved.

There are very many sexual symbols, as well as ibex, seals... and penguins.

In 1994 the EDF (France Electricity) produced a representation of the cave in 3D virtual images.

freezing; do not forget a windcheater.

This trip around the calanques follows an accessible and sumptuous itinerary: the paths may be steep, pass through scree, and involve several rocky projections which may be easy but which are exposed. One should not be afraid of heights. Access is from the Castellane square or the Prado roundabout. You can also take bus 19 until its terminus, La Madrague de Montredon.

Near the transformer, the N°1 blue track climbs up in the direction of the Béouveyre summit. From there, one descends to reach the Chèvres pass, and then take the green N°1 track which goes down to the south. After the passage du Pain, one reaches a vale and follows the yellow N°3 track – dotted; this leads under the Hermit cave, follows the climbing rocks and passes through a breach, the Demi-Lune passage, from where one can see the sea and most of the calanques. The yellow N°2 path goes below, in the north-easterly direction, to descend into the vale and then climb up again towards the Galinette

A thriller in Marseilles

When you are not from Marseilles, neither heart nor body, the reality of this city escapes you, envelops itself in its veils of false pretences, suffuses mists which sap the strong savour of grilled sardines, the odour of the breeze and the choppy sea. The trilogy by Jean-Claude Izzo, Chourmo, Total Khéops *and* Solea, *is composed of books written in the black ink of the city. All the wines which are drunk in these books are duly listed, all the bistros are swarming with people, all the dishes sound appetising – and the town of Marseilles itself is sumptuously drawn. In his works, Izzo recounts the Marseillais universe, describes its vices and virtues with a pen dipped in desire and despair; a writer who gives one pleasures and shivers.*

pass. There is a small cafe at the Calanque de Marseilleveyre. The customs officers' black N°2 track, together with the GR, follows the sea towards the east. After the Podestat calanque, take the green track descending towards the Escu calanque via an open corniche, the corniche des Pêcheurs, then a downwards passage, the Bénitier passage. Once it has approached the Escu calanque, the track follows the edge of the sea, goes above the exit of the purification

The calanques are beautiful but fragile. Attacked from the sea in summer, and by hikers for the rest of the year, they need respect and love.

A *flight* over the calanques

The shore is not a mass of sterile and empty rocks. There, where there remains a bit of earth, and even there where there is only rock burned by the sun, dozens of vegetal species take hold. here are some of them:

The Alep pine (Pinus halepensis), which is able to install itself anywhere.

The onosis has cushions which spread into the hollows, and nothing frightens the coronilla, as long as it can find cracks to house its green and golden tufts. Also well known is the kermès or scrub oak (Quercetum cocciferae) which prickles the legs a little, then the hogweed (Sonchus) which is easily satisfied, and which scatters little spots of purple and gold over the cliffs. There are more than nine hundred vegetal species growing in the calanques, out of the four thousand listed in France.

There are also rare animals, some dying out: the peregrine falcon, the eagle owl, the Bonelli eagle and the Cestoni bulldog bat, the biggest bat in Europe.

of a jug of cool rosé wine, since the route is long.

Climb up to the top of the ridge on the GR in the south-east direction; after a steep descent, here is the Renard pass, then Morgiou and the last bistro before the night.

The second day it is essential to start out early. It is also the path which requires the most physical energy. Once one arrives on the plateau, one finds a wide track, the red path, which heads towards the south-east, to pass again above the Pierres-Tombées calanque. Little by little, the path descends towards the sea and becomes increasingly narrow and eroded. A short climb leads to the Jockey-Club passage, then to that of l'Œil-de-Verre (Glass Eye) where it is advisable to be roped together. This name was given to it because of the presence of an eye painted on the wall. Here, it is best to recover one's breath, before climbing the Vierge vale by a steep path which becomes a chimney. The path then redescends by a steep scree slope towards the Charbonniers pass. The GR then follows the edge of the Devenson cliffs which at certain places rise to a thousand feet above the sea. After passing above the Eïssadon calanque, the track descends into the Oule vale and turns north, to climb up to the Oule pass on the right. It is interesting to make the return trip on the blue path up to the En-Vau belvedere, to look at this calanque from above. It is the best known, and one of the most beautiful. Next one arrives at a little pebbled beach, often in the shade of high cliffs frequented by a multitude of climbers. Here, the GR takes a path where one uses one's hands almost as much as one's legs. The plateau is 500 feet higher up. Previously it was thickly wooded, but was devastated by a fire which started in the heart of the calanques and only stopped at the first houses of Cassis. Finally here is the Port-Pin calanque where one can bathe for a final time before Cassis. The last calanque, Port-Miou, situated at the edge of Cassis, serves as a marina.

Half-an-hour from the centre of Marseilles, the marvel of the calanques, or creeks.

plant of Marseilles – disgusting if the wind is blowing towards you, but the view is astonishingly beautiful. One climbs and then descends the Cortiou pass and then arrives at the Sormiou calanque, where the road from Marseilles passes.

One can take a rest at Sormiou have a bite to eat in the little bistro on the port: the fish are superb here, and the terrace fresh and charming. But one has to resist the temptation

The Crêtes corniche, at Cassis.

A unique vineyard in an exceptional site

At Cassis the cliffs are the highest in France, cape Canaille throws itself out into a sumptuous Mediterranean.

It is at Cassis that the grapes ripen under the sun's paint-brush stroked by the marine breeze.

The bay, the calanques, the hills crowned with pines filtering the Mistral, which arrives in the vineyards without its legendary aggressiveness.

In brief, it would really be a shame if, with all this bounty the wine were poor... but this is not the case, the Cassidian vine gives very fine bottles. It sends its roots down deep into the Cretaceous limestone, to drink the water collected in the subsoil.

After 3,000 hours of sunshine annually and a clement temperature without any brutal variations, the slopes benefit from the influence of a fabulous micro-climate. The Cassis appellation was defined, recognised and protected by decree from May 1936.

With a lightly grilled fish caressed by a trickle of olive oil, a leaf of basil at the side, to breathe in the perfume, wine from Cassis is drunk with pleasure and... moderation.

Cassis...

... which one receives like a "fist in one's face", as Churchill said, offers itself with its finest graces when arriving by sea: all blue waters and white cliffs sprayed with pines. Cassis is a town made for taking one's time on the terrace of a cafe, for pottering around peacefully, looking at the port, and window shopping...

There is an enormous coming and going of boats for exploring the calanques... the climate is almost African, every day is beautiful, a town where it would be good to live.

The "dolce vita" at the port of Cassis.
Photo: Eric Cattin.

The wine from Cassis unfolds its pearly savours and radiates all the sun absorbed between sky and sea.

Something from Saint-Exupéry

On September 26th 1998, the captain of a trawler from Marseilles, Jean-Claude Bianco, fishing between La Ciotat and Marseilles, brought up as usual various waste and debris apparently without any interest from the bottom of the sea, mixed with fish, near the calanques. Before throwing the unwanted objects back into the sea, the fisherman noticed something unusual. This something, scratched, turned out to be a silver chain bracelet hooked to a piece of metal. On this was the name and first name of Antoine de Saint-Exupéry, the first name of his young wife, and the name and address of his publisher in New York.

Several years after the war, a German fighter pilot – reader of the works of Saint-Exupéry! – had produced a military document concerning an American plane which he had sent down in flames over the Mediterranean ("brennend über See" according to the flight report), on July 31st.

Based on French witnesses who had seen the battles in the air or the anti-aircraft batteries firing, and other indices, certain authors had estimated that the crash had taken place off Nice, and in 1994 under-water research was carried out, but in vain. Others thought the place was near the coast of the Var; the hypothesis of the Marseilles shore was put forward but did not seem very credible. Coming back from a previous mission, Saint-Exupéry had returned via Italy. Certain hypotheses attributed the loss to the German aviation, others to anti-aircraft artillery, the formidable Flak. Saint-Exupéry's chief, the French general Gavoille thought he might have had a heart attack since Saint-Ex was old (44 years) for piloting a Lightening and still suffered from the sequels of several serious problems. Only the lifting and study of the wreck could possibly bring more information.

Perhaps the place of the crash was in the waters near Marseilles.

The **Giono** route

Manosque
Salagon
Forcalquier
Ganagobie
Sisteron
Banon
Redortiers-Le Contadour
Limans
Simiane

« *The sun is never so beautiful as the day one sets off* »

Jean Giono

The perched villages with their medieval charm, their old narrow sloping streets, narrow and paved with gutters which circle round taking covered passages and staircases around the old buildings in grey stone, the rustic Provençal beauty of the keeps, chapels and convents, this Provence about which Jean Giono talks is not a real region, with defined limits.

Jean Giono's works turn around this Provence with the austere, bare and brutal face of the high plateaux, territory where the solitude, silence and wind dominate any manifestation of life.

Lyric and poetic, he looks at the rich plains; at the fine juicy orchards, the stone villages, men and their spiritual quest. But he regards this from above, the viewpoint of a magician who carries words to their dumb incandescence, to their point of no-return. Giono's land is a universe linked to the great Mediterranean classics, to Virgil, Homer, and the infinite fields quivering with the silver of the olive trees so dear to their works, to

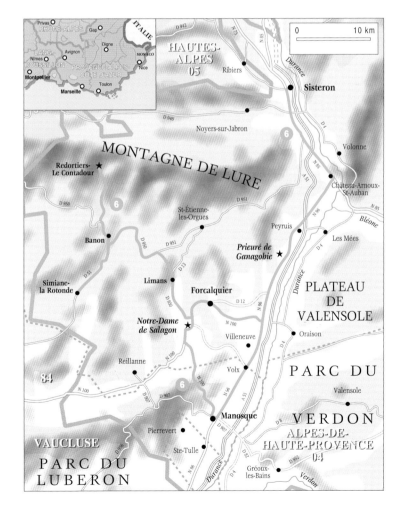

Sites for contemplation and strength: Giono made his characters travel in an archaic and visionary world. Opposite, the Montfuron windmill.

The shepherd, a Biblical figure often encountered in Giono's favoured land.

the arid hills beaten by the sun and rain; the world of antiquity is here, told with words which are not of today, nor of yesterday, but which are still the words of tomorrow.

Jean Giono was born at Manosque, on March 30th 1895, son of a shoemaker from Piedmont and a mother who took in ironing. Since his death in 1970, his works are becoming more and more appreciated. The little village of Manosque haunts his writings, and the land and men of upper Pro-

vence become, under his pen, an "imaginary South" which can easily be superposed on the reality of this region, suffusing it with a quasi-mystic aura.

In order to help his parents, the very young Jean Giono had to leave school and became a bank employee. His magnificent culture is self-taught and he was interested in everything. The success of *Colline* and *Un de Baumugnes*, in 1929, convinced him to live out of his pen.

Giono's beautiful countryside.

He praised his native village, which he never left, Manosque with its four hills; its simple life, that of "Jean le Bleu".

Then the life of the valleys in *Un de Baumugnes*, that of the plains which inspired *Manosque des plateaux*, and that of the arid mountains evoked in *Regain*. The site of Le Contadour, the ideal model for the brotherly community, is described in *Que ma joie demeure*.

Manosque

"Here in front of me the hill of the Mont-d'Or, that of Toutes-Aures, that of Espel, the district of Savels, Saint-Pierre, Moulin-Neuf, Champs-des-Pruniers, the slopes of Manin, Gaude, Sainte-Roustagne, the Adrets, the Séminaires, Pétavine, the Iscles, Le Pont-Neuf, Pimoutier, Champs-Clos, the Soubeyran... The reality, the land which is in my blood. And, moreover, from this everything begins in imaginary lands. But the railcar stops. And here it is, Manosque" (*Noé*, Jean Giono).

The town of Manosque, an important centre of the Alpes-de-Haute-Provence, with about 20,000 inhabitants, is located in the rich Durance valley, at the crossing between the Marseilles-Alpes-Italy and the route linking the Luberon to the Verdon gorges and the Valensole plateau.

Manosque, encased between the hills at an altitude of 12,600 feet is a delightful town.

Walking along its coloured narrow streets and stopping in typically Pro-

Provence, Manosque and Giono...

" *(...) The undertow of the roofs was flattened by the uniform white light; perhaps a light shade indicated the differences of level from one roof to another...*" (Le Hussard sur le toit).
"*Look eastwards and then to the north, and we have seen everything; the country around us is like a sugared water melon, and we are in the middle like the seeds*"
(Manosque des plateaux).

Manosque.

A heart which beats strongly in a peaceful town.

An artisan writer

Giono's father was a shoemaker, and the writer always admired his work. For Giono, a writer is also an artisan. "Liberty means having a profession which you like and which you know. Work like this is leisure. You can therefore produce real works of art. The greatest artistic achievements are the simple works of loving artisans" (Jean Giono, Ecrits pacifistes, Gallimard).

The Jean-Giono Centre.

" In Parais (his house in Manosque) he worked regularly and obstinately. Even his most lyrical passages were written slowly, with reflection, at the rate of four to eight pages a day. He knew that a writer is an artisan, who has to deepen and diversify the techniques of his métier, and that words, rhythms, colours and style must be chosen scrupulously" (Pierre Citron, Giono, Le Seuil).

The Parais house, high up in town, is open for visits one day per week; the death of his wife, Elise, in 1998, left a huge empty space in this well-loved house, and the daughter of the writer returns often.

The Giono Centre, where experts study his works and the analysis of his writings, and where very interesting exhibitions are open to the public from the world over, is a very beautiful building outside town, for all those who, one day, have been excited by the lyric and deeply human prose of this great writer.

vençal squares, where it is good to rest awhile under the shade of the plane trees, is a moment to live and enjoy without hurrying. Depending on one's pottering, around a square, here is the Saint-Sauveur church from the XIIth century, the Notre-Dame-de-Romigier church also from

The sounds of water and drawn-out evenings in Manosque.

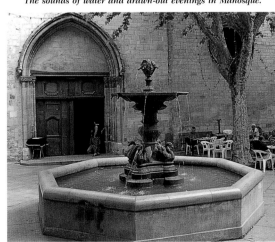

the XIIth century, and the Saint-Pancra-ce-de-Toutes-Aures chapel.

"Manosque is a town of convents, a town with hidden gardens, yards, wells and magnificent fountains" (*Provence*, Jean Giono).

Arriving in Manosque, in a pretty countryside full of lavender and olive trees, one should not miss the Salagon priory which can be seen in all its beauty, warm and light-coloured stone standing out in the landscape. It now belongs to the Département and houses the Conservatoire of Ethnological Heritage of Haute-Provence.

The former Benedictine priory of *Salagon* comprises a XIIth century church, a prior's dwelling from the XVth century and buildings for agricultural purposes dating from the XVIth and XVIIth centuries.

Built on a site which is witness of two thousand years of history, Salagon was an agricultural exploitation in the Gallo-Roman epoch. It was christianised in late Antiquity, with the creation of a Christian cemetery and a basilica, between the Vth and VIIth centuries, and has been completely restored. Inside the church one can now see a beautiful fresco from the XIVth century.

The Salagon Conservatoire is a research centre, a museum, an exhibition and an animation site. The medieval garden exhibits plants used before the great discoveries, collected together according to a composition and organisation in a draught-board pattern in the spirit of monastery gardens. The medicinal herb and ruderal garden displays plants from the Lower-Alpine pharmacopoeia and flora used in the inhabitations of Upper Provence.

The perfumed garden offers its collections of lavenders, sages, mints, artemisia and umbellifers...

Other theme gardens are planned: an ecological garden, a collection of willows, market gardens, magic gardens...

Left:
One of the Manosque gateways, the Saunerie.

Right:
Salagon has been completely restored, and its market gardens, planted with medicinal herbs and essences, are open to curious visitors.

Forcalquier, the old capital of Provence.

The city of the "four queens" is still a stopping place for kings.

Forcalquier

These days, Forcalquier is a beautiful little town, sub-prefecture of the département; it was not always like that. Beautiful, certainly, but at a certain time it was also powerful, the capital of the whole of Provence...

In 1125, Forcalquier became the capital of the county comprising the dioceses of Apt, Sisteron and part of those of Gap and Embrun.

In 1214, the county was reunited with France; the title of county of Forcalquier was namely carried by the counts of Provence and then by the Kings of France until Louis XVIII.

And then the town was also called the "town of four Queens" since Count Raymond Béranger, who lived there between 1200 and 1245, married his four daughters to four Kings: Marguerite married Saint Louis, King of France; Eléonore, Henry III, King of England; Sancie, Richard de Cournouailles, Emperor of Germany and King of Rome; and Beatrix, Charles d'Anjou, King of the Deux Siciles.

However, this episode came at

the end of long and bloody wars of succession certain of which put Provence to fire and blood.

The arrival of Louis XI, the Wars of Religion, the epidemics and then the Revolution marked the decline of Forcalquier. All of this remains evident in the stones of its monuments, inscribed in the palaces and the old dwellings with sculpted wooden doors. The old town, whose alleys climb under covered passages, staircases and squares with fountains, is very picturesque.

One must visit the Cordeliers Convent, founded in 1236, which suffered many depredations during the Wars of Religion and the Revolution. The interior chambers and the gardens, designed by the Franciscans, have been very well restored.

The citadel which overlooks the town, and which can be reached on foot by taking a path shaded by huge trees, is dedicated to music, as indicated by the statues of angel musicians surrounding it. There is a charming tradition according to which each evening at 7 p.m., from the 17th to 24th December, the "Nadalet" – or Little Christmas – is interpreted with the carillon rung with fists, as in the old times.

A curiosity of Forcalquier is its "campo santo", a very fine cemetery with pruned and shaped yews, a listed site inscribed in the Historic Monuments Inventory.

Left:
A complete history behind an old closed door.

Right:
Sensuality of fruits and vegetables, round and juicy, at the Forcalquier market.

Notre-Dame-de-Provence.

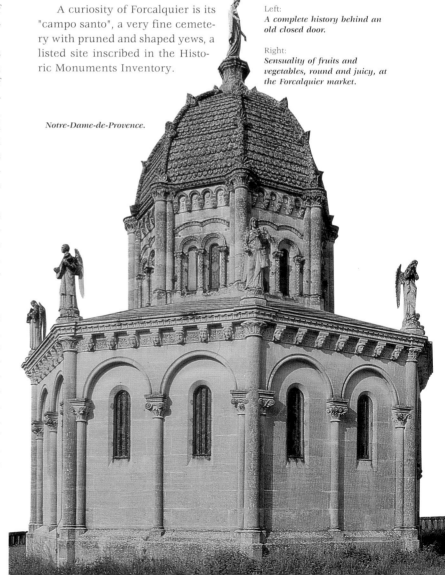

Portal of the Ganagobie priory, an admirable Clunisian abbey.

Oneiric animals and myths revisited; the Ganagobie abbey mosaics have been restored recently.

The **Ganagobie** priory is the high-point of a majestic belvedere, a magnificent observation post over the river Durance.

Before arriving at the wonderful Clunisian abbey, one comes across a borie (stone hut) which adds it own sense of antiquity to this site, which is a real natural monument.

The church with its single nave, Provençal Romanesque style is doted with one of the most beautiful porches in Provence, superbly decorated; a recent restoration revealed mosaics from the XIIth century, of oriental inspiration.

The priory was founded around 930 and attached to Cluny Abbey around 950, when Saint Mayeul was Abbot. The monks were chased out by the French Revolution; the church and cloister were partially destroyed in 1794 while the monastery had been sold as a state possession in 1791.

A hundred years later, the owner donated it to the Benedictine community of Sainte-Marie-Madeleine, settled in Marseilles.

After lengthy restoration work, in May 1992, it was installed in the renovated and extended priory in order to be able to accept all the monks.

Sisteron

"Silence, solitude, the play of light and shade on the earth, the violence or gentleness of the wind, the perfume of the air, the pure water, the echo of the vales, the divine disarray of intelligence confronted with simple things, the architecture of mythologies. Here, nothing is pre-digested, everything is in its original state, the essences are intact. The earth, water, sky, fire are for you alone. The landscapes are personal; for certain of them, yours is the first eye to see them" (Jean Giono, *Provence*, Gallimard, Folio).

If the town of Sisteron exists, it is because of the last glaciations. The glacier advancing from the north met an immense mountain ridge which still extends from Gap to Mont Ven-

toux. At the site of Sisteron, the rocky block which was not very thick there ceded and a passage opened to Provence, an open door to the Mediterranean.

Throughout history this strategic situation brought about long battle episodes at each invasion. Sisteron, fortified and protected by its citadel was often at the heart of numerous wars, particularly during the Roman invasion of Augustus in 27 B.C. From the Roman era, the "Segustero" exists, the vestiges of a mausoleum and a city along the "Sinistra Way" which linked the Aurelian and Domitian Ways. After the succession troubles of Charlemagne, Sisteron passed from hand to hand: local viscounts, Forcalquier counts, then Provençal counts, before finally being

The Baume rock, at Sisteron. Material for "mythological architecture".

*Sisteron, the town of silence,
gentleness, echoes.*

attached to France in the reign of Louis XI.

The Wars of Religion left the town in ruins.

From whichever angle one regards Sisteron, the first thing which catches the eye is the citadel. Perched on its rock, through its majesty its fortifications still seem to protect the town spread out at its feet.

Banon

"On the slopes facing the Durance valley one finds the village of Banon. Between the two, solitude" (Jean Giono, *Provence*).

Second commune of the country for number of inhabitants after Forcalquier, Banon is the only passage to the Albion plateau and, beyond that, the Vaucluse. Legend has it that the name Banon comes from the word 'bane' which means the sprouting horns of a young goat.

Coming from Forcalquier and arriving at an altitude of 2,800 feet, one can see that the fine fields of lavender, the generous pastures and the soft curves which relaxed the eyes have changed into a

Where do the santons come from?

At Sisteron, there is an exhibition of mangers and santons every year, in December and January: this is for the Melchior prize, the prize for the best "santonniers".

The santons, which appeared in the XVIIth century, are little biblical figures shaped out of terra-cotta and painted. Previously, they were used to decorate the Christmas cribs: the shepherd, the hunter, the simpleton, the pistachio nut drier, the drunkard, the woman carrying wood. They came to offer their gifts to Jesus. This artisanat developed during the Revolution, a tumultuous time when the churches were closed. The inhabitants celebrated Christmas at home, and each family had its own crib and manger. The oldest santons are in faience or wax; and have become collectors' items.

rough landscape, Pre-alpine. Sharp ridges and sombre vales, with a river which hides itself, the Calavon, and which helps feed the waters of the Fontaine-de-Vaucluse, just a crow's flight away: this is the environment of a village made famous because of its cheese and whose medieval enclosure, a sort of crown, makes this impression of austerity even more vivid, "a wasps' nest" as Giono said.

However, the air is pure and exhilarating, the houses with their blue shutters, balanced delicately between beauty and melancholy, the people, laughing behind their beards, no longer completely Southern, already mountain people.

One small curious note: the stones from the Banon quarry pave the pyramid of the Louvre in Paris.

Banon, the "wasp's nest"
as Giono called it,
looks more like a bee's nest.

Below, left:
At Fontaine-de-Vaucluse,
a column dedicated to the
memory of Petrarch.
An amazing little town
to be visited, preferably,
out of season.

The "banon" of Banon

The region extending around Banon is still very marked by the breeding of goats. The short grass with concentrated savours and the recipe refined over the centuries mean that a very well known cheese is produced here enveloped in sweet-chestnut leaves. When one has eaten these exquisite marvels in Banon, one notices that the same cheeses elsewhere do not have quite the same taste... Advice to gourmets, the banon is to be eaten fresh, soft, creamy and dry..

Simiane-la-Rotonde.
A sunny village,
open and full of charm;
one would like to live here...

Redortiers-Le Contadour

A village made up of two hamlets, Redortiers and Contadour, a place of solitude and silence. The atmosphere is exactly the same as that evoked when reading a page of Regain, the book inspired by these ruins, and these rather sad houses. The writer owned an old sheep-fold in Contadour. There is a little chapel dating from the XVIIth century, a town hall isolated between the two hamlets, and all around, the sharp and cutting atmosphere of a land at the end of the world.

Limans

"The pigeon house in a field of lavender".

This very old site shelters the remains of an oppidum from the year 919. To the north it still has its Middle Ages fortifications, and at the southern gate, ramparts and a tower. The oldest houses in the village, dating from the XVIth century, have low doors – 5 feet high – with wooden lintels. Later buildings have keystone lintels. The village fountain dates back to the XVIIth century; one can see an ingenious system for using the water in successive stages. The Saint-Georges church, listed, dates from the XIVth century and contains a palaeochristian altar.

All around the village, the famous pigeon houses: some of them date back to the XVth century. On the heights, the Ybourgues hamlet, a fortified farm from the XIIth century occupied by the Knights Templar, between the Laye and Limans dam.

"The belfry, rotunda, the low walls, the undulation of the roofs

around him were like trees, shrubberies, hedges, and the hillocks of a new land" (Jean Giono, *Le Hussard sur le toit*).

There is a mysterious rotunda overlooking Simiane, a small old town with great character at the western edge of Forcalquier country, within the Apt country, perched on a rocky spur of the Albion plateau, and built in terraces. This village, together with Lurs – Manosque country – and Trigance – Verdon country – is one of the jewels of Upper Provence.

It is difficult to describe the ensemble. This is the charm of this high-perched village, of its harmony.

One enters the medieval village through the upper portal: on the right is the house of the novelist Ponson du Terrail. Climb up the narrow alleys, and you cannot fail to admire the massive doors set with diamond shapes, the lintels in dressed stone, and the houses dating from the XIIIth and XIVth centuries with chevronned façades. From the terrace of a good country bistro in the vast covered market there is a superb view. Finally, one arrives at the Rotunda, a keep from the XIIth century, one of the most beautiful and strange monuments of Upper Provence. This building was part of the defences of the fortified castle of the Agoults de Simiane. With its height cqual to the width of its base – nearly 60 feet – it is hexagonal from the outside and decagonal from the inside. The main room is situated on the first floor; its acoustic qualities are such that a well-known classical music festival has been held here for the past fifteen years.

A country bistro

In this beautiful country, there are astonishing bistros, well placed, as at Simiane, really good, as at Saumanne. With their old-world charm, these village cafes are all discovering a new life, offering a local daily menu, together with an atmosphere which was on the verge of disappearing. This is doubtless the pleasantest way of meeting the local inhabitants, learning about their customs, and the art de vivre of this region.

**Simiane:
the rotunda.**

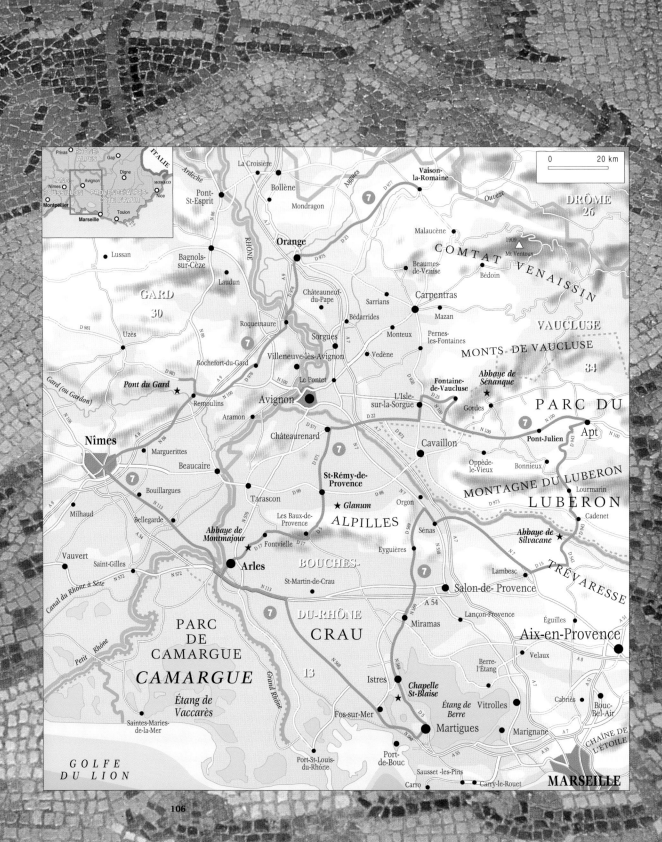

The Ancient Provence Route

A little history

Until the VIIth century, Provence was inhabited by the Ligurians, probable descendants of the autochtone Neolithic populations. Then there were Celtic infiltrations and the installation of the first Greeks. Massalia – Marseilles – the oldest town of France, founded in 600 or 620 B.C. by the Phocaeans from Asia Minor – a fortified site dominating the natural creek of the Lacydon, was taken. In 1967 in Marseilles, the garden of Vestiges was discovered, near the present Old-Port, and holds ruins dating from this era. One see the horn shape of the ancient port here, since in those days the sea came in much further than now.

The mixing of populations which shaped Provence was born at that moment. These peoples settled in their "oppidums", the upper sites: Nages, near Nîmes, Saint-Blaise above the Gulf of Fos, Entremont near Aix, all began their cycle as real towns.

Vaison-la-Romaine to the north, Nîmes to the west, Aix-en-Provence to the east – Caius Sextus Calvinus founded the town which bears his name, Aquae Sextius – and the Mediterranean marked the limits of ancient Provence.

Massalia very quickly became a powerful merchant city, relying on Glanum, Avignon and Cavaillon. Up until the IInd century B.C., the autochtones and the Phocaean city lived together in understanding, and then the different Provençal peoples started to kick over the traces against the "imperialism of Massala". Between 125 and 117 B.C., Marseilles called on Rome for help. Entremont was destroyed and Aix was born. Romanisation accelerated under Augustus and in 27 B.C. Antonin the Pious, from Nîmes, took over power. This epoch marked the apogee of the Gallo-Roman civilisation. In Rome, luxury and ostentation in all aspects of daily life became an *art de vivre*; this could be seen in the architecture, the decoration of the houses and the arts in general. It was the same in Provence, as expressed in

The Roman Art de Vivre

The remains of the very rich houses of Vaison-la-Romaine, which have resisted because of the materials employed, stronger than those used to build the more modest dwellings, date from the IInd and Ist centuries Before Christ.

They comprised a succession of covered and uncovered spaces, offering views over the rooms and the colonnades of the porticoes. When they were inhabited, these houses were magnificently arranged and decorated: plays of water and wells of light, interior gardens and statues.

Carpets, furniture and art objects, which have disappeared today, rendered the interior of these villas welcoming and precious.

The building rules were precise and practical: the kitchens, for example, were located to the north, so that food could be conserved better, the hearths and the baths were situated close to an entrance, so that it was easier to feed them with wood, while the bedrooms were usually on the first floor, where the heat rose, and were of restrained proportions to keep up the temperature of the rooms.

Since it was impossible to heat the whole of the house, an ingenious system of hot air circulation was organised from the caldarium and the tepidarium of the baths. In order to avoid draughts, the windows were closed with plates of glass. The big entrance doors were closed in winter by a system of sliding panels made of wood; one of these door sills with a groove can still be seen in the House of the Dolphin, at Vaison-la-Romaine.

the many remains which are still visible. The IInd century, which saw the arrival of Christianity in the region, marked great political changes, the decline of Nîmes and the abandon of Glanum, whilst Saint-Blaise, higher up and better protected, was occupied more. In 392 the edict of Théodose forbade paganism. This was the end of the polytheist religion of the ancient Celtic-Ligurians. The end of an epoch.

Vaison-la-Romaine

The huge public edifices which have been preserved make it possible to imagine the size of the city, estimated at 150 to 170 acres. There is a theatre carved in the rock of the Puymin hill (I[st] to IInd centuries). It could hold 5,000 to 6,000 spectators. Today it is a wonderful site for the Summer Festival held there.

A temple from the era of Augustus stood further east. It was a public

Below, left:
Entrance to the house called the Silver Bust, at Vaison.
Below, right:
The Pompey portico, at Vaison.

The theatre of Vaison-la-Romaine, the present site of the Summer Festival.

edifice with a religious vocation. The remains of several baths are visible in different places: to the east of the paved road on the Villasse site, the so-called South baths on the right bank of the Ouvèze, those of the North built in the middle of the Ist century stretch over 2,000 square yards. The oldest are inside the house of the Silver Bust. The heart of the city, formed by the forum and the basilica, is not known, since it is buried under the present town. Only a fifth of the original town has been excavated.

On the southern slope of the Puymin hill, one finds objects and inscriptions which help to understand the life of ancient times. The most interesting pieces are huge marble statues, those of the three emperors: Claudius (41-54), represented with the civic crown of oak leaves. Domitian (81-96), as war chief, and Hadrian (117-138) idealised as a hero: he has the beard of a Greek philosopher, the imperial princely cloak and

The statue of Augustus, at Nîmes.

The baths at Vaison.
Remains which are evidence
of the exceptional standard
of the way of life
in Ancient times.

Orange

Ancient Orange – Aurasio – is famous for two monuments: the theatre, an extraordinary framework for Choregies, and its triumphal arch.

The theatre has the same dimensions as that of Arles, but it leans against the hill, which meant that is was easier to build.

Inside, the edifice is almost complete, but one should imagine it with the decor which made it famous in the ancient world. The hemicycle could

a crown of laurel leaves. There are also models of the theatre and the House of the Dolphin, objects from daily life, frescoes and magnificent mosaics found in the Peacock villa. The Peacock mosaic was originally in the dining room.

The hemicycle of the theatre at Orange
- opposite and detail -
could hold up to 9,000 spectators.

hold up to 9,000 spectators, and was divided into three zones.

From the top of the tiers, one can verify the perfect acoustics, one of the most appreciated qualities of this theatre.

The triumphal arch, which stands at the north entrance to the town on the ancient "Via Agrippa" is one of the best preserved antique monuments in Provence. Built around 20 B.C., it celebrates the exploits of the veterans of the IInd Legion, since in 40 B.C. this town was their colonial residence.

Left:
The triumphal arch of Orange, magnificently preserved.

*The Pont du Gard,
a spectacular construction
dating back to 40 A.D.*

*The Square House
at Nîmes is not a house,
neither is it square...*

Pont du Gard

This is the grandest part of an aqueduct which used to carry water to Nîmes from Uzès. This bridge, built around the year 40 A.D., and which has resisted the floods of the river Gardon for two thousand years, is one the marvels of Antiquity. The three levels of arcades are recessed one on top of the other. The total height is 160 feet, and the upper level is 900 feet long.

Nîmes

The arenas in Nîmes, built between 50 and 100 A.D. are doubtless the best preserved monument from Roman times. Inspired by the Coliseum of Rome, this amphitheatre was essentially used for battles between gladiators. The originality of the edifice and the ingeniousness of the ways of access made it possible to control a huge influx of spectators. In the Middle Ages the role of the arenas was changed so that it became a strong hold with dwellings inside, and the first corrida was held in 1863.

The Square House is not a house and it is not square. It is in fact a Roman temple 82 feet by 40, of Greek inspiration, which at first was dedicated to Augustus and then to Caius and then to Lucius Caesar. The latter were considered the princes of youth and became the symbols of Nîmes. This temple, built towards the year 5 A.D.

The Fontaine Gardens at Nîmes. The structure and layout are inspired by the gardens of Antiquity.

had other functions throughout history: a place of assembly, a dwelling, a stables, and a church.

These days, the Square House holds art exhibitions and finds itself in a contemporary setting since the building of the modern "Art Square" mediatech opposite.

The Fontaine Gardens

Located at the foot of Mont Cavalier and overlooked by the Magne tower, the Fontaine gardens were the first public gardens of France, laid out in 1750: before this date, gardens were just ornamentations for châteaux. The style is typical of the Age of Enlightenment: vases and balustrades in stone, statues of fawns and nymphs, peaceful terraces and basins emphasised the evident inspiration of Antiquity.

Here, one finds the famous Nemausus spring and the Temple of Diana, another monument dedicated to a divinity.

Below:
The first corrida was held in the Nîmes amphitheatre in 1863.

The theatre of Arles, built under the reign of Augustus at the end of the Iˢᵗ century B.C.

The Magne Tower, at Nimes.

The Magne tower

On the top of Mont Cavalier, after crossing the Fontaine gardens, one reaches a tower which has not yet revealed all its mysteries. It is octagonal in shape, and it is said to be a mausoleum, a watchtower, a place of cult worship, or even a lighthouse, modelled on that of Alexandria.

The Temple of Diana

Within the Fountaine gardens, not far from the basin, is a monument which is one of the most enigmatic. It has not been possible to discover its original purpose, even though some think of a sauna or a library. The edifice is partly destroyed but remains magnificent, with its vaulting with juxtaposed arches, its columns and cornices.

The Notre-Dame-et-Saint-Castor cathedral

The building is to be found in the centre of Nimes, on the Place aux Herbes. Dating back to the Roman era, it was destroyed and rebuilt several times. It is a wonderful example of early Languedocian Romanesque art. The particularity of this edifice is a frieze representing scenes from the Old Testament, decorating the façade.

Inside, there is the tomb of the famous Cardinal Bernis, favourite of Madame de Pompadour and dead ruined by the Revolution.

Arles

Arles was the neighbour of Ernaginum, the cross-roads of two Roman roads, the Domitian Way and the Aurelian Way. Because of the Rhône and its strategic position, this town became first of all a powerful colony and then an imperial residence and Prefecture of the Gauls under Constantine, from the IVᵗʰ century.

The theatre was built under Augustus at the end of the Iˢᵗ century B.C. It is not as well preserved as that of Orange, and the stones used for its construction were re-used by the Arlesians for other buildings. The 335 foot "cavea" could hold up to 10,000 spectators and the stage was decorated with statues; the Venus of Arles is displayed in the Louvre Museum in Paris.

The amphitheatre dates roughly from the same epoch as the theatre. It was later transformed into a fortress, and a real little town was built inside,

The Arles amphitheatre.

until about 1830. At that moment, the antique monument was uncovered, which measured 446 feet long and 350 feet wide, and which could hold 20,000 spectators.

The Constantine baths, or rather what is left of them, were just a small part of the ensemble built between the forum and the river Rhône.

At that time the town possessed baths to the South, under the present Republic Square. These baths were in a way the reserve of the emperor Constantine, and therefore very luxurious. In the Middle Ages, stray animals were shut in there. *Sic transit gloria mundi.*

The Alyscamps, a famous necropolis which has been written about very often, stretched along the Aurelian Way and was installed outside the walls. At a certain time, at the end of the IVth century, the inhabitants of Arles did their best to be buried here.

Below, left:
Arles, the arena.
Below:
Arles, the Constantine baths.
In the Middle Ages,
stray animals were shut in here.

Saint-Rémy-de-Provence

Glanum, in the Alpilles, became Hellenized in contact with Massalia. Its apogee came in the IInd century B.C. Under Augustus, it benefited from prestigious public monuments, but was later dominated by its neighbouring city, Arles, and faded in the I[st] century A.D. The most spectacular sites date back to Antiquity: the triumphal arch (I[st] century B.C.), and the mausoleum (35 B.C.) are among the best preserved Roman monuments.

In this naturally beautiful site, enclosed in an almost wild ravine, indenting the Alpilles plain, archaeological exploration, started in 1921, has revealed several successive layers of occupation: dwellings and public buildings from the Glanics before their subjection to Rome and prestige urban settings from the Roman era (temples, forums, public baths...).

The vestiges of these two civilisations coexist and mix together, forming a spectacular documentary treasure.

Even though a first occupation of the site goes back to the I[st] millennium Before Christ and there are several traces from the VIIth and V[th] centuries B.C., it is the edifices of the IInd and I[st] centuries B.C. and those of the I[st] century A.D. for which Glanum is famous. Situated at the exit of a gap in the Alpilles chain, Glanum was at the

The splendid site of Glanum, at Saint-Rémy-de-Provence.

cross-roads of two ancient Ways linking Italy and Spain (one via the Alps and the other by the shore). This privileged position gave it an important place in overland trade. Besides, water sources were abundant and there was a recognised "cure" spring. The indigenous divinities, including the god Glan and the mother goddesses, were venerated by the inhabitants, the Glanics, a branch of the Celtic-Ligurian Salians.

We know more about Glanum from archaeological excavations than from written sources. In the IInd century B.C. the habitat and the public and cult edifices in dressed stone developed. The Greek influence can be felt

in the architecture (fortified porch and ramparts, nymphaeum, temple, square surrounded by porticoes, assembly hall, luxurious houses organised around a courtyard) of this sanctuary town where the Glanics struck their coins. Even after the Roman campaign of 123 B.C., this monumental centre was not abandoned, but on the contrary was rebuilt to become bigger and more prosperous. After 45 B.C., with the foundation of the Roman colony in Arles, important architectural and urban changes transformed the sanctuary and gave it the essential characteristics of a Roman town. Abandoned at the end of the IIIrd century A.D., in favour of Saint-Rémy, the town served as a stone quarry for the builders of the new agglomeration.

The complex aspect of these ruins, and the presence of several successive stages, forces the visitor to make an effort. Consult the models, plans and aerial photos at the visitors' centre, which distinguish four zones for the visit.

The ravine

A path descends towards the Alpilles ravine whose entrance was defended by a fortification of huge bonded stone blocks. The wall, supported against the rocky counterforts to the east and west, was topped by crenellation. A complex entrance system demonstrates the strong defensive aspect. Dedications to Glan and the mother goddesses can be seen near the sacred spring. On the other side of the road, a staircase leads down to a very deep basin of a spring which justified the ancient cult. Framed by bonded blocks in limestone like the staircase, it was covered, as shown by an arch in dressed stone (partially rebuilt).

Agrippa, son-in-law and minister of Augustus, built a temple overlooking the source, to the goddess of health Valetudo, as shown by a dedication engraved on the big stone blocks. To the right of the corridor leading to the source, a statue of the god Hercules with its inscribed base and six stone altars are still in place.

The central zone

The monuments of the 1st century A.D.

– the forum (one of the oldest in Gaul). One can see the moulded base of the outer wall, in the centre of which was a paved square, very damaged, bordered by two porticoes with colonnades, closed at the northern end by the basilica used for civilian purposes. Two annexes opened in its north wall contained a building with an apse (curia) and a chapel dedicated to the imperial cult;

– a triangular area forming an intersection with a portico of the

Doric order, a monument with columns, a monumental fountain and a paved platform whose purpose has not yet been identified;

– two temples called "the twins", parallel, of different sizes, each set on a podium, of the Corinthian order and prostyle layout; an elevated gallery (peribolus) surrounded them, defining the sacred domain. An attempt at restoring them has been made to give an idea of their height and appearance.

The monuments of the IInd and I[st] centuries B.C.

THE LOWER DISTRICT

The public baths were built here in the triumviral epoch (around 40 B.C.), and two stages can be distinguished. They have a big courtyard (palestra) bordered by three galleries. To the north, the three rooms for ablutions: cold, warm and hot. To the south, the swimming pool. North of the baths, there was a residen-

Left page: *Glanum, the foutain.*

Below: *Glanum, Basilica.*

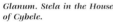

Glanum. Stela in the House of Cybele.

Right:
An atrium at Glanum.

Right page: *Les Antiques. Detail of the western side of the Mausoleum (right)*

tial district, including the Epona house which revealed artisanal installations. Under one part of the baths, an ancient house with peristyle and mosaics. To the west, several other houses occupied from the IInd century B.C. to the IIIrd century A.D., without their layouts changing very much. The oldest walls were built out of bonded stone blocks, while the most recent are in irregular quarry stones. Thus one can see the house of Cybele and Atys, and the Antes house. The quality of building is further proof of the prosperity of Glanum and the taste for the luxurious way of life of the Mediterranean peoples.

LES ANTIQUES

Marking the road crossing the Alpilles, the triumphal arch (first quarter of the I[st] century A.D.), today without its upper part, announced the northern entrance to the town by evoking the conquest of Gaul by Rome. Following the different sides, one can see sculpted panels with conquered women and warriors from Gaul, or Rome atop a pile of weapons and a Gallo-Roman pointing out a

Les Antiques. The west of the Triumphal Arch.

vanquished Gaul. Developing this ideology, the garland of fruits, and winged Victory's in the spandrels playing trumpets.

The Mausoleum (about 40 B.C.) of the Julii family, a noble family from Glanum, is dedicated by three Roman citizens of this family to their father and grandfather. It has three floors: a sculpted cubic plinth whose mythological scenes (cavalry battles, foot soldiers around a dead warrior, a wild boar hunt, a combat against an Amazon) recall the events in the life of the heroized defunct; the next stage is a triumphal arch with four doorways emphasising the link between these exploits and Caesar's victories; finally there is a round chapel encircled with columns which shelters the statues of the two defunct wearing togas.

The ensemble of the collections of the town can be seen in the museum of Antique Arles. Among these treasures, there is a sumptuous collection of sarcophagi from the IVth century and a collection of ancient sculptures and mosaics, together with Augustean statuary of Hellenistic inspiration. The contemporary architecture (Blue triangle on the peninsula) adds to the spectacular site, next to the Roman circus where excavations are under way to find other riches.

Julian Bridge. What is the explanation for the niches which pierce the structure from side to side?

The Julian Bridge

This bridge which spans the Calavon – or Coulon – on the ancient Domitian Way, comprises three arches. Its two piers are pierced by openings which allowed water to pass through in times of flooding.

Marseilles

From Massalia to the little Rome of the Gauls: 26 centuries of history. Around a ship from the IInd century, the wreck of the Bourse, discovered in the ancient port, the Historical Museum has organised its collections on the foundation of the Phocaean city and the Greek town. Behind the town hall, the Roman Docks Museum displays remains from the Ist century A.D. and a series of amphora.

The Archaeological Museum of the Vieille-Charité presents, apart from an Egyptian collection (the second in France after that of the Louvre in Paris), an exhibition of the remains of Roquepertuse (IIIrd century B.C.), painted and sculpted fragments.

Left:
Marseilles. The horn shape of the ancient port.

Right:
*Marseilles.
Roman Docks Museum.*

122

Saint-Blaise

Saint-Blaise is situated between the Berre Lagoon and the Gulf of Fos. This oppidum, inhabited in Neolithic times, was abandoned between the 1st and 4th centuries A.D. A great number of Etruscan and Greek amphora were found here, which seems to show that Saint-Blaise had significant trade links with nearby regions.

The ramparts, as well built as those at Glanum, date from the same epoch and were probably constructed by the same builders. There are signs on some of the blocks, marks which could have been sculpted by the workers to indicate where they should be set during the construction. Saint-Blaise was probably abandoned after the siege in the 4th century, and the cannon-balls found among the remains seem to support this thesis.

Ramparts at Saint-Blaise.

The mysteries of the Fontaine-de-Vaucluse

The opening of the Fontaine-de-Vaucluse.

Once you have left your car in one of the parking places of the little town, you have to walk for ten minutes to discover the site of the fountain. In order not to be afraid and not to want to turn back immediately, you should choose a moment in the year when it is not too busy and a day which is not too sunny. Only under these conditions does the famous green, turquoise and jade water of the fountain have the possibility of humming its enchanting songs. Under sheer cliffs 1100 feet high opens the abyss where the mysterious resurgent spring appears. In fact, the variations in level cannot be explained by climatic conditions nor by other natural causes.

The source has been explored many times. The first time was by Ottonelli, who descended 75 feet in a diving suit, in 1878. Cousteau himself went down to 242 feet in 1955 and in 1985 a remote-controlled submarine reached 1010 feet, landing on a sandy floor.

As for experiments on the colour of the waters, they have proved that the river Sorgue collects infiltrations from over a very extensive territory.

The castle of Fontaine-de-Vaucluse.

Below: **The water which surges from the spring is an astonishing colour and very clear.**
Lower right: **The mill wheel of a paper factory turned by the waters. The plant still produces sheets of different grades, and its speciality is to include flower petals.**

Bibliography

TRAVEL CHRONICLES, NOVELS AND PRACTICAL BOOKS

In the basket: books to take with you on a journey in Provence :

Daudet (Alphonse), *Lettres de mon moulin.*
Colette (Sidonie Gabrielle), *La Naissance du jour.*
Colette (Sidonie Gabrielle), *Prisons et paradis.*
Durrell (Lawrence), *Spirit of Place.* Leete's Island Books, New Haven, Connecticut.
Giono (Jean), *L'homme qui plantait des arbres.*
Giono (Jean), *Que ma joie demeure.*
Maupassant (Guy de), *Sur l'eau.*
Pope-Hennessy (James), *Aspects de la Provence.*
Van Gogh (Vincent), *Lettres à Théo.*

For the library and the reading corner :

Binet (Françoise) et Racine (Michel), *Jardins de Provence.*
Delange (Yves), *Le Jardin familial méridional.*
Forbes (Leslie), *A Taste of Provence.*
Forrester (Viviane), *L'Enterrement dans les blés.*
Jouveau (René), *La Cuisine provençale de tradition populaire.* Nîmes.
Lequenne (Fernand), *Olivier de Serres : agronome et soldat de Dieu.*
Mauron (Marie), *Le Printemps de la Saint-Martin.* Paris.
Maurières (Arnaud) et Rey (Jean-Marie), *Le Jardinier de Provence et des régions méditerranéennes.*
Mayle (Peter), *Une année en Provence.*
Mistral (Frédéric), *Mémoires.*
Noailles (vicomte de) et Lancaster (Roy), *Plantes de jardins méditerranéens.*
Pagnol (Marcel), *Manon des sources.* Paris.
Pagnol (Marcel), *La Gloire de mon père.*
Pagnol (Marcel), *Jean de Florette.*
Pagnol (Marcel), *Le Château de ma mère.*
Pickvance (Ronald), *Van Gogh in Arles.* Metropolitan Museum of Art, New York.
Romilly (Jacqueline de), *Sur les chemins de Sainte-Victoire.*
Stendhal (Henri Beyle, dit), *Mémoires d'un touriste.*
Wentinck (Charles), *Provence : mythes et réalités.* Arles, Editions Bernard Coutaz.

L i s t o f

contents

Front cover :

Simiane-la-Rotonde.

Back cover :

*Harvest time near the Dentelles
de Montmirail.*

Martigues

Sénanque Abbey

Gordes

Olive at Les Baux-de-Provence

The Geants' Way Roussillon

Frigolet Abbey

Graphic design: Hokus Pokus
Cartography: Patrick Mérienne

© Édilarge S.A., Éditions Ouest-France, Rennes
Cet ouvrage a été achevé d'imprimer par l'imprimerie Pollina (85) - n° L95286B
I.S.B.N. 2.7373.2449.1 - Dépôt légal : mai 1999
N° d'éditeur : 3837.03.4,5.01.05